This book is dedicated to
all the little green men —
I know you're out there!

My Diary

Intimate secrets of neighbour
Dan Falzon

Everything you need to know about
Australia's most delicious TV star...
and more in his own words

B🌿XTREE

Published by Boxtree Limited, Broadwall House,
21 Broadwall, London SE1 9PL, 1995

With special thanks to Myfanwy E. Marshall
for her help in coordinating this project.

10 9 8 7 6 5 4 3 2 1

A CIP catalogue entry for this book is available from the
British Library.

ISBN: 0 7522 0113 1

All photographs and artwork from Dan Falzon's private
collection except for:
Paddy Engelen: pages 84; 59 *bottom*
Grundy Television, Channel 10: pages 6 *bottom*; 8; 30; 31;
32; 34; 40; 55; 64; 65 *bottom*; 74; 76 *bottom*; 77; 81; 85
Myfanwy E. Marshall: page 6 *top*
James Morgan: pages 60 *top*; 72 *top*
Jim Moyes: page 83
Serge Thomann: pages 9; 11; 12; 13; 15 *top*; 21; 26; 32;
33; 43; 44 *bottom*; 45 *bottom*; 49 *top*; 52 *top*; 63; 65 *top*;
73 *bottom*; 75; 76 *top*; 88; 89; 91
Shout: Front cover and page 5
TV Week: page 44 *top*

Photographs by Paddy Engelen, James Morgan and
Serge Thomann supplied courtesy of
Idols Licensing and Publicity Limited

While every effort has been made to credit the work in
this book correctly, the publisher apologises for any
regrettable omissions and will gladly correct any errors
in future editions

Cover design by Shoot That Tiger!
Book design by Dan Newman

Colour reproduction by Jade Reprographics
Printed and bound in the United Kingdom by Cambus Litho Ltd

Dear Dan,

Hi. I'm a really big fan of yours. You always make me laugh and brighten up my day. My walls are plastered with posters of you and I videotape all your scenes from 'Neighbours' and watch them over and over again.

I want to know EVERYTHING about you. Are you anything like 'Rick' in real life? Because I think he's just the coolest character and livens up the show heaps.

What's it like growing up in Australia? Is it really like on 'Neighbours'? Are you friends with the other stars? Do you have a girlfriend? What sort of girls do you like?

Is it true you're a greenie? Did you always want to be an actor?

So is it fun being famous? Tell me about an average day in your life?

I read in a magazine that you always reply to your letters, so I'll be waiting.

Lots of love from your number one fan,

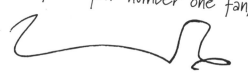

P.S Please send me an autographed photo, preferably in your bathers (Speedos?)

P.P.S I love you lots.

14 April 1995 On tour, UK

What's all the fuss about?

Dear Number One fan,

G'day. Thanks a lot for your letter. I was really touched by your compliments. It's good to hear you're not using my posters as a dart board. You're right about replying to letters. I've always tried to respond to all of them but it's a bit difficult lately because there are literally thousands and I'm in between meetings, recordings, films... you name it. But I do my best (sometimes, haha).

So, you'd like to know all about me would you? Well, where do I start? Let's see. I was a typical Aussie kid, livéd by the beach, I played sport with my two brothers, watched *Neighbours*, one day I auditioned, got a part and here I am!

Only kidding. If only it was that simple. There's a lot of hard work involved, and a bit of luck in the beginning. SO, WHY ME? Who knows?

I've never been one to like talking about myself, but... since you're my number one fan... (well, only one)... I'll give it a go.

A typical day in my life, hey? Well, I can give you a taste of my diary... let's have a look here:

> hectic day, feeling exhausted, got mobbed, signed a couple of thousand autographs, my hand was about to drop off... (they must have thought I was someone famous).

Yeah, it's pretty full on and it's steadily getting busier. Life has changed quite a bit since my days on *Neighbours*. I've been on tour for almost two and a half months now, living out of a suitcase. Today for instance, began at 6am. Now, why was that? Where was I this morning? It's so busy I can't tell one day or place from the next. OK, I remember. At 7am I had a live TV interview in Scotland on *What's Up Doc?* and have been going from one appearance to the next ever since. This tour is covering mainly England, Wales and parts of Scotland. Right now I'm on my way to the 24th, and final, wee appearance for today.

They've got me in this huge stretch limo at the moment. I prefer perching up high in my four-wheel drive thanks. There are heaps of fancy gadgets inside here, I'll give it that. They're fun to play around with. Mmm, what's in here? Aha! Drinks. Real Scottish scotch. Check. Oops,

Typical politician – hand over the baby.

broke it, they don't make eskies like they used to. I nearly blew up the speakers cranking up my Pearl Jam CD. I don't think Henry was too impressed (that's my friendly neighbourhood chauffeur.) Ah yes, music, the only thing that keeps you sane. I love this line, it's a classic 'I change by not changing...' sounds good to me. Pearl Jam are legends.

Tomorrow is full of meetings, including one with my music producers. I am laying down some tracks next week with my band, which I can't wait to do. Then I fly home to Australia and take care of some other work for my company and see my family and mates. I rang Kimberley Davies (alias Annalise) a while ago on my mobile. I caught her just as she'd finished a scene on location (Ramsay Street). It made a nice diversion for Kimbo to hear a running description of the Scottish countryside as I'm passing it. Ah yes, it's a steamy day back home, she's quick to point out, while I'm freezing my butt off! Thanks 'KD'. But, I'm having a ball. She laughed when I tried to imitate a Scottish accent. I'll make a wee call to mum next. Aiy.

Oh oh, here we go, just rocked up... there are crowds everywhere, can barely get through the gates. Must be somebody important coming. Nope, can't see anyone. Watch out Henry, we don't want any broken toes! Stevo just perked up because of all the beautiful girls. Gets him every time. I'm still recovering from being in a human washing machine (mobbed) an hour ago. If it wasn't for the minders I would have said goodbye to my jeans, ouch. Silly hey? But it's just part of the job. Yesterday's venue was cancelled because they were lacking crowd control (security).

One, two, three, four... yep 12 police here. We've hired two extra security, so including my own, all up there are 17 guys looking after me. (Didn't think I was that much trouble). The crowds are massive. It's chaos, the police escorts are trying to break it up so we can get through. Here come some girls with big signs.'We love you Rick'. Ah, here's one with *my* name on it. There's the BBC, they've heard about the fiasco. It's on for the young and old! Catchya when it's all over.

DASHING DAN... the star and his minders get set to leg it from his mobbed car to the safety of the shop

Dan's Trip to Rammy Street...

AUSSIE soap star Dan Falzon left hundreds of screaming Scots fans in a lather yesterday.

The Neighbours heart-throb caused a near riot after cutting short an autograph session. And many of the 300 girls, who'd waited FOUR hours, didn't even catch a glimpse of the teen idol! One heartbroken fan, 10 year-old Julie Croxford, was left in tears after the visit. She was crushed in the crowd and bundled out of the way by Dan's team of heavies as they fought to get him inside a

15th April 1995

Hi again, just had a four-hour sleep and my minder took me training – a one-hour jog then a workout at the hotel gym. I was going to get back on my guitar and play a few chords to relax a bit, but then I thought I'd use the time to write before we're on the road again.

I suppose you're wondering about *Neighbours*. Well, I've got *Neighbours* to thank for giving me the fantastic opportunity and apprenticeship into the industry. It's been due to the show that I first hit British screens and how you came to know me as a 'neighbour'. But you wanted to get to know me didn't you, not Rick. So how did Dan become Rick? I'll tell you, but first I'll let you in on a little secret of mine.

I grew up with *Neighbours*. The show that is. Back when Kylie and Jason were the stars I had a feeling that it was not just another show. But maybe every Australian kid felt the same.

If I had kept a diary back when I was younger it would have read something like this:

It was a weird thing, but I always knew I'd be on *Neighbours*. I've never spoken about it publicly. When it happened, I'd known for years beforehand. I just knew somehow I was going to have a connection with it. Sounds really strange I know. When it actually happened it was like, OK, it's happened – time to work! And what a lot of work it was! A really full on job, but I had an absolute ball.

Having great fun on my summer holidays. Went boogie boarding at the beach with Tom and Ben. The surf is really strong, nearly got wiped out. Came back to Dad's spaghetti Bolognese tonight. I pinched the last few snags (sausages) and blamed it on Big Brother Ben. Got away with it. Hee hee. Watched 'Neighbours'. Charlene and Scott were having a fight. Something weird about that Ramsay Street place. I don't know how, but one day I reckon I'll live there too. Much as I love it at Mum's and Dad's, I just feel like I belong in Erinsborough.

Left to right: Brettles; Eliza; me; Marnie; Troy Boy and Peter.

Most of my teenage years were spent on Ramsay Street, in the public eye. But where I grew up was quite different. There are plenty of ups and downs in the biz too, but it is such a fascinating industry that people tend to only see the glossy side. I'm not saying behind the scenes is bad; there's just so much involved and a lot more depth than often shown. It's taken me on a wild journey which I'd love to share with you.

It's a long way from my peaceful days back in Mount Martha where I was raised. (I was originally a country boy). Yeah, when it all gets a bit much I just reflect back there – with my family, the surf and the view of the beach from our house. My earliest memory which sticks the most is running through the trees with my brothers.

Time out.

Mum and Dad used to put us through long walks up to the pine forest plantation on the hill where there were miles of trees, hundreds of feet tall. It was just like walking through giants' legs. Within the darkness of the forest, I can still remember how the only light came from the sunbeams filtering down through the tree-top canopy. I can still smell the fresh scent of pine. The ground was covered with pine cones, and wet bark and moss-covered quartz rocks. We'd dodge the pine trees and rabbit holes as we'd run. We'd just run for miles. We were brought up to run. Sometimes we'd play hide' n'seek and chase each other in there. It was an amazing place, our own magical world, just ourselves and the wildlife running around. If we were lucky we'd catch a glimpse of a rabbit or a fox scurrying away, most probably from us – the human predator.

Sometimes we'd just sit and listen to the thousands of birds singing away in the tree tops – rosellas, kookaburras and an occasional wise owl making tunes together that are now packaged and sold as relaxation music.

I never felt any danger there whatsoever, just very comfortable and peaceful. It was such a heavenly place. I remember growing up having that freedom. I have that freedom within me now, but I still long for that same space, like when I went hiking in Scotland on my day off from the tour. I need that. It's a breath of fresh air for me. Great thinking time, but back then it was a way of life. Even at a young age, I felt it was home. Each smell, every astonishing view, from the delicate insects, to the larger marsupials, and the whispering trees, they were all a gift, not to keep, but for all to enjoy. That forest meant an enormous lot to me. I thought it would stand tall forever, but during the time I moved to the city with Mum, the area was logged. Wiped out. Gone forever. Angry, hurt and bewildered, I vowed to always help protect such places, primarily for its inhabitants and delicate ecosystems, but also to carry and preserve these gifts so my children and their children can also experience the magic.

With that seed in my mind at six or seven years of age, I remember understanding the problems that were going on in the world – like deforestation and pollution. In addition to this was my love of animals and so my first real dream was to become a park ranger, to play my part and look after the land.

I grew up wanting to be a park ranger.

Hey, this is isn't so bad. I usually find talking about myself really boring. Are you asleep yet? I've always written journals and poems, though now I've turned to lyrics. I guess it's easy for me to talk about my childhood, it was great. I could talk about it forever, especially about the environment, it's one of my strongest passions.

Mount Martha

Mount Martha is a beautiful place located around a bay along the coast of Victoria, surrounded by countryside. It's about one and a half hour's drive south east of Melbourne. I lived there until I was seven but then I only visited when I saw Dad after my parents divorced. We used to run down the hill for a half-hour jog and come to the only shop – a servo that just had a milk bar and a big ice-cream sign out the front near the petrol tank. Every summer the city kids would come down and hang out there. We were the locals, so it was quite weird to see this strange breed of kids, so different from us innocent little country folk.

Mount Martha has grown so fast and has completely changed. Back when I was a little kid, there would have been just a couple of hundred people. I remember seeing the whole hill green one day and the next time I looked out, houses were spread out everywhere. Boom!

Speaking of booms, I can hear the crowds outside going berserk (maybe it's on a loud speaker). Looks like the limo just arrived to take me away. I'll have to pick this up later. Catchya.

My ranger days.

Some time in July

G'day. Back again.

Sorry about leaving this for so long but I haven't had a chance to keep writing as I've been pretty busy with recording tracks. I've only just touched down in Oz. I'm at Dad's place for a few days, so there's some time to write. I have heaps to tell you about everything that's been happening, but first, I'll take off where I finished.

Now, where was I up to? Oh yes. Mount Martha. Well I'm actually sitting up in the second storey of the house which looks out on to the beach, so it's the perfect time to describe what it's like. I've been up here visiting Dad and jamming on the guitar, writing a few songs with my brother. The view is a fantastic inspiration.

The sea is deep blue, just like the sky. It's been a sunny day. Not bad for winter. During summer there is a special feel and is something maybe only

Australians can understand. In the afternoon when it's getting dusk there's a beautiful warm breeze. The crickets start chirping, the insects buzz, the frogs have a go too, and the birds start singing loudly together. One kookaburra starts up and the rest get in on the act. But it's just this breeze that blows over you. It's so calming, nothing beats it in the world, or nothing I've experienced.

The view from the top storey and deck also overlooks our backyard. It's about an acre and a half and we made good use of it. Mum was always passionate about her gardens. We grew our own veggies and picked fresh fruit off our own apple and orange trees, and all the rest. The goats and chooks made it into a miniature farm. We were always chasing the animals in the backyard, riding motorbikes or playing war games or cops and robbers with weapons we'd made out of wood. We'd just invent our own make-believe games.

At one stage we had an above-ground pool, full of cobwebs and their bugs (good name for a show). Our pool quickly turned into an aquarium. It wasn't funny, we just couldn't control it – frogs, taddies and wigglies, they were pretty cool to try and catch. We grew up with insects and redback spiders. Dragonflies always amazed us, they looked so weird and scary buzzing around, but we knew they'd never harm us. Dad caught huntsman spiders in his hands and let them crawl on us, much to Mum's dislike, but she understood 'boys will be boys'.

The view from my bedroom.

Mum taught us how to read through books like *Mr Men*. My parents are arts teachers so we were drawing as soon as we could hold a pencil. We mostly drew animals and in our paintings there was always a sun blaring down. We drew our world. Mum took us for walks to the bay to pick wildflowers and we'd sometimes draw those. We'd spend hours just searching for shells. We were like water babies. The whole ambience of the sea was part of our world.

We had nature at our doorstep. Looking back now, we had the perfect environment to be nurtured. We had everything and needed nothing.

Being in the country we never used to lock the doors. At night we'd just leave the fly-screen door open, with the sounds of the distant ocean waves floating through. We didn't bother locking the cars either. We felt completely safe.

Brothers

As brothers Tom, Ben and I became best friends because we were all we had. We shared bunks in a tiny room. (This was the case until I left home at 20). Our closest mate was our neighbour Glen. He got us into the band KISS. We thought, 'He must know what's going on'. We were a bit behind the times. So, we suddenly became fans, recording all their songs, wearing all the gear – the hats and T-shirts.

I even had a KISS make-up kit I was given as a prezzie from my parents. I've still got it somewhere. It was such a novelty then, but now make-up goes with my job – not one of my favourite aspects of acting!

I remember going outside and hearing Glen play the drums next door and it seemed really cool. That's when Ben picked up the drums, and Dad taught us the guitar. So it was like, 'Lets start a band one day fellas!'

We were just little country kids with hand-me-down clothes. We always shared our clothes – we still do today when we're all together. That's class! Whenever we get short of anything we're into each other's drawers. I know it's unusual because a lot of friends come over and can't believe we even share the same undies! When I buy something I think, 'I hope Tom likes it'. It's just the way it is with our family.

We used to have a ball getting into trouble with waterbombs. Once we were playing with firecrackers on the roof, and the next thing we knew the police squad were hovering above us in a helicopter. One time we were rolling a tyre down the pathway at the park and it turned and rolled down the hill on to the main road, jumping over the kerb, weaving in and out of the cars. We didn't think a tyre could be intelligent enough to dodge four trees, stay in line with the road and travel non-stop to the next suburb without causing an accident. We just stood back watching it in slow motion with our mouths wide open and then ran. Tom and I were like, 'What tyre? Nothing to do with us'.

My brothers and I were always coming up with money making schemes. At about eight or nine years old Tom and I used to collect all the rubber bands that the postman littered everywhere and then we'd knock on all the doors in the neighbourhood saying 'We're selling these on behalf of the Royal Children's Hospital'. They'd ask 'Oh, how much?' and with that Tom and I produced

Tommy the Tank and me playing pool.

Slamming in the bedroom to Pearl Jam.

two winning identical smiles and say '50 cents each please'. We made a fortune! That'd cover us for a month's worth of lollies (quite enterprising I thought).

We also used to sell newspapers on street corners and compete between ourselves. Then Ben, Tom and I each had a go working at Maccas, alias McDonald's. I used to stuff burgers down my shirt and say 'I'm busting to go to the toilet'. I practically ate all the profits! Then they said to me 'You've got a nice smile. You can serve out front with the girls'. I was forever being reprimanded for not saying what I was supposed to. I figure if they want something, they'll bloody ask me! I was in constant trouble. Some days I was late. Some of the girls who'd felt guilty for stuffing up the balance left the difference under the machine, so I'd be in there cleaning away and cashing in, thanks very much. Ah yes, another Rick Alessi prank – helping himself to the coffee shop till. One day the manager said 'Dan – it's all over, you're out boy! You no-hoper!' I laughed in his face and walked out cracking up.

Mum and Dad were great cooks. Mum still admits today that Dad taught her how to cook. He is great with pasta sauces. He came from an ethnic background, Malta, where they have a variety of dishes and they're cheap to make. Malta is like Italy and Greece, places renowned for hearty meals. Food is of such an importance in their life, whereas today's life is a quick takeaway, or microwave TV dinner. They find the time to sit down as a family and *cherish* everything.

I love sitting down talking to people and dining. When we were kids we all sat down together at the table, talking about the day's events – who shot who in the backyard, who cooked the butterflies (just kidding). I think communities just don't seem to talk anymore, you just don't know the person who lives next door to you for ten years!

We were very lucky in Mount Martha. We all grew up in a very tight community, with a school where all the kids interacted. We were always playing cricket out the back and we'd walk into the neighbour's backyard – like in the show. I see the show *Neighbours* as a Utopian society. If that represented true life in any country, it would be a beautiful thing just to walk into your neighbour's house, say 'G'day', go straight to their fridge, chat over a beer and solve each other's problems. That would be unreal.

Family

Family and friends are really important to me. No-one knows me better than my family and I know I'm lucky to have two great parents and two great brothers who stand by me. I can always rely on them when I need some help and I'd do the same for them. I know there are kids out there who don't have great parents or brothers or sisters. Fans write to me about the hard times they have at school and their drug problems. I think that without a community it's difficult for kids to open up and go to places where they can bond with other kids and share their experiences. It feels like there's this huge lack of trust with everyone. Not many people know their neighbours these days.

Grandfather

My grandfather sailed out to Australia from Malta by himself after he'd just married my grandmother and worked until he could get enough money to bring his family over. My dad had just been born. He did odd jobs around Melbourne and then moved to Sydney and worked on the railways in the Blue Mountains. Over the years he put money into property, but his whole life was focused on looking after his family, so he took this 'mad' trip to make a new start for his family. Those sort of things don't happen too often these days so I admired him for that. He was an extremely resourceful man. He could single-handedly build houses and fix cars. He worked hard so his family could have a plentiful life. Maltese people are very close and family orientated and that's where my base comes. People find it weird how Ben, Tom, and I are best mates as well as brothers.

THE INSIDE STORY
TOM

I guess I bring him back a little bit from his madness from doing so much. Because we are all so close, he makes an effort not to get on the wrong side of us. He doesn't want to be a brother who ends up who knows where, so we don't see him.

Maltese people are supposed to be romantics, from that sort of Mediterranean world, and very women-orientated. I'll have to ask my mates to comment on that one for you. Maybe later.

My grandfather had great faith in education and believed you shouldn't get tied down by things you have to do, rather than want to do. We all took on that philosophy.

He was always one for good deeds. He was a builder, Dad told me how he'd build someone's extension and Nunna would say 'where's the money?' He'd say, 'don't worry about that, it might come', he'd done a good deed and somewhere along the way it might be rewarded. He died a few days before Christmas in 1992.

THE INSIDE STORY
DAD

On the day of my father's funeral, he came to my rescue. I had to deliver a eulogy and Dan could see I was getting emotional. Out of his own convictions he came up to me and said, 'Do you mind if I say something?' That was the best thing he could say. I said 'Dan take over' and he came up and talked about how his grandfather was such a strong and good man.

Karma

I have so many beliefs I come back to. I believe in karma, that what you do in life all comes back to you. If something happens like backstabbing, or someone goes out of their way to hurt you, it's so nice to think that it will all work out. It could be twenty or thirty years, but it always comes back to them.

I come up against people every day who are very economical with the truth. They will lie to me, or they won't give me the full story so I will do something, for example where publicity is concerned. Photographers say particular shots won't be used and then they pop up on covers. It's a dodgy business. You soon learn. Having a base of truth gives you full respect for yourself and having a clean slate no one can ever bring you down.

I believe you do create things by being positive, it creates powerful vibes no matter what happens. Negative things just bring you down. You've got to shake them off. There's no point in getting aggressive about things. I remember Dad saying years ago, it's all very well to fight in the school yard, but it's the man who tends to walk away from a fight who comes out the winner.

I stick by the morals that I was brought up with. Dad tells us 'enjoy yourselves, by all means, just don't hurt too many people along the way'.

I'm not religious. I see religion as a strength for people to hold on to and if it works for them – great. I'd never disrespect people's beliefs. We're all different. I guess I have my own strength that come from my beliefs, from karma to being honest. It sounds almost childish but it's very true. The truth is very powerful.

Home sweet home

Our home at Mount Martha is a large white weatherboard house, full of spider webs all over it, so now it's turned into a sort of grey. It's positioned on a hill so the house is split-level. Dad built on the extension which is upstairs with the deck. The house is worth a lot more now than when mum and dad bought it for $16,000 in the early seventies. It's now worth so much more it's not funny. The area has developed and real estate value has sky rocketed. Economically it is an asset, but it's home, whatever it's worth. Wouldn't sell it for all the money in the world. The world changes so much these days it's nice to have a place you can still call home, that you were actually brought up in. That's a luxury. It's my private hideaway.

Ghosts!

One night in the house I had a strange encounter.

I was alone, Dad was away. I was sleeping in the room where strange things had occurred before, but they didn't enter my mind at the time. I'd just jumped into bed, it was a still warm night, when suddenly I heard a car which came up the stairs to the front door, creating a wind that rustled all the trees. I could feel it coming closer. The noise was becoming louder. The trees started shaking like mad and then the wind came bursting through a closed door in the front room and slammed the door in the next room. I was lying face down and I felt very uneasy in the room, like someone else was in there.

That's when a sequence of knocks started on the wall. Then the knocking stopped for a while and whatever 'it' was started walking around the bed. The door was now closed. I felt like running, but I thought, 'what if I get to the door and it's locked?' I didn't move for hours, I was glued to the bed. I eventually went to sleep. I don't know what or how, but something was in the room that night .

Sitting in the haunted room with my friend Ingrid.

Raelee Hill came up to the house one night with a couple of other cast members for a type of slumber night and she walked outside for some air. She came running back in suddenly scared, she felt there was something eerie outside. I hadn't mentioned anything to her about the house, but the next morning she told me she'd had nightmares.

Tom and his mate were in the bunks one night when they heard a noise coming from a wall. Then they started to feel a presence above their head, a real pressure, which turned to breathing, and then they could actually smell a putrid breath. Tom and his mate grabbed the sleeping bags and sprinted upstairs to be near Dad (don't blame them).

Weird things started to happen when we built the extension in 1988. My parents had moved there in the early Seventies when it was just a cottage once owned by a shearing family. Before that, we were told, it was a site used as a place of rest for stockmen, where they would stop to boil a billy. Who knows? Maybe we were the trespassers.

Growing up

I found the autobiography I did as a Year 8 English project to give you more of an idea about growing up here. I guess the beginning is always a good place to start. This is what I wrote at thirteen years old about the birth of the guy behind 'Rick'.

On my first camping trip.

> ### SCHOOL PROJECT: MY LIFE
>
> When my birth was imminent, Mum started getting very frustrated. Money was short, so she couldn't afford to get her hair done so she took to the scissors and did a hair-style that today's punks would have been proud of.
>
> To Mum's embarrassment she had to go to the hospital like that. My birth was a difficult and long one for Mum. She lived at Mount Martha at the time and needed to spend time in the city, with my Grandmother, as she feared having to be rushed into the city by helicopter or ambulance.

Hippies rule!

Big Brother Ben

The apple of Mum's eye.

My brother Ben was only one year old when I came along. These days Ben is used to having two younger brothers who receive a lot of attention. He's not interested in working in the entertainment industry, but he was the first one acting in primary school. He had his fun and that was it for him. He's got a degree in recreation now and has also done managerial courses. He works in a recreation centre as a fitness trainer and as a life guard at the pool. Ben is the quietest and most placid son in the family. He's kind, like Mum. He's more settled than Tom and me, being the big brother. He's very patient, resourceful and methodical in every job, like the old man. Whereas Tom and I are like – a quick job is a job well done. I certainly admire Ben for that.

My actual birth took six hours from that point at 8.45pm on the 24th of November, 1974. I was a 6lb 9oz wonder.

When I arrived home my elder brother Ben was very jealous of me because I had all the attention.

THE INSIDE STORY
BROTHER BEN

To me Dan is still the same person that he was before *Neighbours* happened. I see him still as my brother, no differently. To us it was just part of his career option. It was great that he got where he was, but to us it was like it's just our brother really, no different.

17

Little Brother Tom

The third boy is Tom, who is eighteen months younger than me. Yep, three boys each almost a year apart. Mum must have been having fun! Many people say Tom and I are like twins and sound similar on the phone. We're very close mates and have the same interests. He does some modelling work, commercials and was recently a presenter on a kids' show in Sydney – *The Zone*. He's multi-talented. He writes well, he's a musician and has always wanted to act. He's sharp with jokes and never stops laughing. All he needs now is to take the same journey I have. It would be great if we could work together one day. (Double trouble).

Tom's a bit of a Romeo. He is about the same height but a bigger build than me as he works out regularly. Ben and I are always laughing at how many girls he has stringing along, something like six girls ringing up in one night! (What about me?)

THE INSIDE STORY
TOM

His friends have been my friends and pretty much vice versa. I think it's the fact that we're such a close age. As brothers there is a lot of loyalty between us. We've been in a few blues, but, I hope it's not boasting to say, we're intelligent enough to realise that fighting doesn't do much for us. Living in bunks in the same tiny room we've learned to get along and we've found we're more productive that way. If we need to avoid each other we just walk out... probably not talk it out, just call each other 'snapperhead' or say 'you're a mess'. But we wouldn't take it deep, we'd just know it's irrational and go and do our own thing.

THE INSIDE STORY
TOM

"Dan's had nights where he's come back from somewhere with his friends and I'd wake up, look in the lounge room and there'd be twelve of his mates all over the floor. I'd come in stepping over girls and guys, going 'how are you doing? I'm just going to the toilet, yeah, Merry Christmas!' But that's also a reflection of our parents, they're accommodating in a sense, they're not going to grudge against anyone.

THE INSIDE STORY
TOM

We catch up with each other when he's at home and say 'How're you going, good thanks, can I borrow ten bucks?'

Who's tough?

Mum and Dad

We called them hippies, but that might be a bit too strong a word. They were alternative though; vegetarians, into Indian type relaxing music and very 'anti' routine. When I found out they were hippies it was the coolest moment in my life.

Mum is my favourite person on earth. She is very caring and perceptive and extremely gentle. She is always smiling and softly spoken. In my eyes she is the best mum. Nothing gets in her way of helping people; race, colour or class. It's a quality I've always admired in her. She is always out there helping people. That's something I hope I've adopted and maintain as a real value. She works as an integration teacher, helping immigrants with a second language. That was moving on from art. She also paints and sculpts. We have a lot to thank

My family: Ben on Mum's lap; Tommy on Dad's and me practising my profile look.

Mum and me in 1995.

19

A communal bath with my brothers, as well as my cousins, Nathan and Hamish.

Mum for, her dedication and devotion. There was never a lot of money in the family, but we always just got by. Mum was in and out of different teaching posts, but she'd always put us first. She supported every venture we did. She had a lot on her plate. The last few years we've all sort of pitched in a bit.

She's a real intellectual, always reading, especially about different cultures. She sees things in perspective. She used to teach yoga and she was a dancer when she was a young girl.

Dad

Dad and the boys in 1993.

Dad is a funny guy. Our friends have always called him Jimmy Hendrix. He used to look like him with his curly hair that went everywhere. My brothers and I used to throw

cobwebs in his hair and he'd never know. We'd end up laughing for the rest of the day watching little spiders crawl out of the leaves in his hair.

He's more of a mate and older brother. Still, being our Dad, he'll always be there for us, but one to one we can talk to Dad as an older brother, as a mate. He always helps us out with cars. Dad's the perfect handy man, if there was ever a job to be done, he knew how. He never needs help from anyone else. His father taught him carpentry, mechanics, you name it. I wish I had a few more of his skills. When Mum

and Dad separated he never passed on the tools of the trade. He'd show me now, if I had the time.

He is an incredibly intelligent man who can always see the bigger picture. Like with Mum, I value his opinion on what I'm doing. We chat on the deck or over jobs like chopping firewood and fixing cars (while I watch anyway).

Both my parents have remarkable personalities and have been very inspiring figures for us. Both are very compassionate about the world's problems, as opposed to the trivial things in life. Mum finds peace in reading and Dad has Mount Martha.

They supported us in everything we did and gave us their time. They exposed us to as many options as they could, like with sport, and watched how it all went, so we couldn't go that far wrong with those sort of parents. I can't remember being spanked once, they just talked things through. Our punishments were like, not going to the beach. Because we have a close open relationship.

SCHOOL PROJECT: MY LIFE

Life at Mount Martha was very pleasant when I was a youngster. Mum had three boys in as many years, so we always had mates. At one stage we had six dogs, six cats, an aviary, three goats and some chickens. There were lots of fruit trees in the big garden, a veggie garden, nice flowers, and great big trees to climb. My Grandfather and Dad built my brothers and I a three storey cubby house with a real fireman's pole.

Top: *Me and Dad on the balcony.*

I loved that cubby. On the third level there was a steeple with a bird house. It was huge. We had dart boards inside and paintings on the wall. It had a corrugated iron roof where we'd sit and check out the view or dry off after a swim. I have a lot of memories in that cubby. I fell and hit my head once (not that there's much to hurt up there anyway), and we'd get splinters, but that's just the Australian way of life, you're always out there getting grubby, with dangerous spiders centimetres away from you. There was no fear.

We also used to have a big oak tree which we called the Faraway tree, based on the book. It was perfect for climbing and right at the top was a beautiful view of the

THE INSIDE STORY
DAD

He'd always be thinking of what to make with the cubby house. It wouldn't be just 'Let's build a slide rope', no, Dan wanted a bloody pool at the bottom of the slide, so you'd climb up dry and land in water. He brainstorms, he thinks like that. He doesn't do the obvious.

whole bay. We used to hang out up there, till Dad chopped it down because it was rotting away and becoming dangerous. So there went the Faraway tree. We sat on its stump and cried.

School

A drop-out. Yep I'm afraid so, bit like Rick hey, but that was the only time for me. Besides, I enjoyed being with nature and chatting to Mum much more. We're very close.

I must admit, I did prefer my older brother's friends to kids my own age. I guess I just liked hanging around the kids who knew more, and could get up to more mischief. My brother Ben was expelled from kindergarten for fighting with the daughter of the owner. (Now that's full respect.) We weren't having a good track record starting off were we?

Community school was great. A lot of schools are very structured, but the Community was into alternative learning. It was based on a hippy idea about sharing communal land. There was one open room built like a ski lodge, complete with log fire and its own kitchen, with about fifty kids mixed together, from grade 1 to grade 6. Kids taught other kids. They used a process of learning that was based on fun, so that each lesson was not a task. Each week

MIDYEAR REPOR

DAN FALZON   GRAD

Oral language good – able to

LANGUAGE   Written language improving.

Have found phonic

vocab from language

Progressing well. Has only

cesses, but good grasp

concepts, classification

contributes extensively when

of activities/areas if not

and able. Good eye

y. Can plan ahead, a

originality. Grasps

es movement + creat

se of rhythm :)

terested and capak

ring his own physica

Is relaxing with me;

shows this. Works we

Dan is eas

needs to be

of reinforcement. I

r, quick to help othe

BALCOMBE
PRE SCHOOL
1978

there would be a different theme that would be applied to all subjects, so we'd do plays, write poems, paint and take bush walks as part of the curriculum. There was maths as well, but the subjects weren't pigeon-holed.

The school was also very creative arts orientated, and had a stage and crafts area in the room. It was based on the family, as an extension of the home. All the parents were rostered to help run it. The kids would have working bees, planting trees, so it was our school, that was a way of kids taking pride in their school. There was also a lot of support from the adults, the kids knew there was always a parent to talk to. The parents made soups and bread on Fridays and would sell them at the market for school funds.

First kiss

My first kiss was behind a tree. Her name was Samantha. My mates were talking to her mates all day. It was really exciting, but nerve racking. They threw us together in the end. (OK, maybe I didn't need a push.) A peck on the lips and that was it. That was love. Ring the bells, name the day, we're getting married! Ha ha. Then I ran home. She was beautiful.

> I have always been very fit and a good runner. I remember Mum telling me that I ran so fast if I didn't watch where I was going, I would run right into the trees.

Running

Yeah, the amount of times I smashed into trees running, I couldn't tell you. It lost me a tooth one day (try explaining to your mates that a tree knocked you out). Somehow, Dad got us into running marathons with him. I was about six when we started. Sometimes in the long races we'd join in half way through, so we could finish with him. It was never anything seriously competitive, it was all just for fun, although we put 100 per cent in, it was never do or die. That's what we grew up believing – you learn from winning you learn from losing, and that's the basis of everything.

Running has now simply just become part of my everyday life. Fitness is important to me. You feel more alive when you exercise. My Dad taught me it's a real discipline keeping fit.

Divorce

I remember the day when Mum and Dad split up, that was the actual day that we left Mount Martha.

It was like, bang! We looked at each other and then we were gone, just like that. Dad sat there and watched us go, we waved; 'Seeya Dad'. In the car we asked where we were going and what the hell was going on (in kiddie language), and were told 'We're going to stay at your grandparents for a while.' It was like, 'Oh, cool!' We were confused. We knew maybe Mum and Dad weren't talking to each other, but we never discussed it, we just accepted it. We understood there was a problem and they were fixing it, but we didn't discuss why. Mum said 'You'll be going to visit your father once a fortnight', and we did for years, every other weekend. Dad would pick us up in the yellow Combi, still going

> 1981 – my Mum and Dad split up. My grandfather came down to Mount Martha and picked up my Mum, my brothers and myself, and took us to the city, where he and my Grandmother lived. I was six when I attended Errol St Primary School. I had a very bad first day. It was a new school and a new teacher and I didn't want to leave Mum. We had to be pulled apart, and I went to my new class screaming.

today, and we'd head back up to Mount Martha. We were close to Dad, but at the end of the day, Mum was always the one looking after us.

The actual split never worried us, still doesn't to this day. We have never once thought it would be great if they got back together. I haven't pursued finding out why they split because my parents are the two happiest people I know. Mum being one of the most beautiful people I know, and Dad, like an older brother – cool, what else do we need?

Bringing us up, Mum always put us first and she has always looked after us 110%. We were always first. Wherever we went we stuck together and looked after each other. We stayed at our grandparents for about a year and she bought a house of her own in Melbourne where I lived until I moved out in early 1995.

Beginning Grade 3 was just as uncomfortable as beginning kindy. This is what I wrote about fitting in:

SCHOOL PROJECT: MY LIFE

1983 – In 1983 I did grade 3. My teacher that year was Ms Halsal. The grade I was in seemed uncomfortable at first because I was with kids that had all gone to kindergarten together, and had been in the same grades since then. All their parents were either working at the school, or on the school's committees. Sometimes, I felt like I was the odd one out. After a while I got to know them better and we became friends.

Below: Á la carte breakfast. That's class!

One of the camping trips we made that year was to a beautiful nature reserve called Blackwood Forest. My family have always loved camping and whenever we could we packed and went. It was very hard for us to put up the large tent, but usually someone helped us. I have always loved rainforests and animals, and trips to places that had either were always good. At Blackwood Forest, we camped near a creek with millions of mosquitoes buzzing around. The next morning my brothers and I chased some kids off, because they were throwing stones at a goanna in the tree.

Goannas are big lizards, a bit like miniature crocodiles. Don't squirm. They're not that bad! Cute little critters really, that wouldn't hurt a fly. Well, except when they're eating them. But seriously, they wouldn't hurt anyone so why should why they be hurt ?

My brothers and I spent the first half of the holidays with Dad again at Mount Martha. While we were down there we started playing a lot of tennis. We also went boogie boarding and listened to music. The experience has always been really nice, of waking up and hearing birds chirping outside your window, and not having any worries about school. We also did lots of swimming that holiday, and played some badminton.

The second half of the holidays we went to Queensland for the first time with Mum. We were flying for the first time as well. It was such an unusual feeling when we took off, because the plane goes on such an angle, you feel like you're going to fall out of your seat. I loved to look down at the clouds, and the tiny houses and matchbox cars.

Back on that first plane ride I never would have guessed I'd be flying as much as I do now. On average I fly from Australia to England at least five times a year. These days I jump on planes as if it's no different to a train, except I still get a buzz being up in the sky and looking down at the clouds. It's another world up there and a feeling of freedom. I was once asked if I was an animal, what would it be? I answered a bird, something like an eagle who could soar up high in the sky and look down at everything. I'd just spread my wings and go.

We arrived at Coolangatta Airport, and caught a bus from there to Surfers Paradise. We were staying at a place called the Beachcomber. I thought it was such a luxurious place because of all the facilities. We also had a great view. My big brother Ben and I stayed up one night to watch an electrical storm over the sea. We went to a place called Grundy's every day, because they had millions and millions of electronic games. It wasn't long until we had to depart, but I wasn't too disappointed, because after all, we were going back by plane again.

Greetings from the Vagabonds.

DECEMBER 1977

We used to call it the yellow esky — we figured it would be great to fill it up with ice and a couple of beers...

1984 — In 1984 I was doing Grade 4, my teacher was Miss Ramsay.
Our whole grade put on a play that year. It was called Swan Lake.

1986/7 — We took the bus to Queensland, and it was a lot of fun. We saw beautiful countryside and stopped every three hours at service stations for refreshments. It took one and a half days to get there.
Seacrest. There were many young people staying at the apartments and we quickly made many friends. Every day, we went down to the beach, to ride on our boogie boards. The weather up there was just great. Every day 30 degrees Celsius.

Melbourne

Our home in Melbourne, where my mother and two brothers still live, is a house with a tiny backyard, much smaller than what we were used to at Mount Martha, but we had a big playground next door in the park. We would play hockey, soccer and footy there, and next to the park was the zoo. Thanks to the zoo we didn't have to miss the animals we'd grown up with in the country. After school we'd get in free. At breakfast time or when it was just getting dark, the monkeys would be screeching and the birds would be going off too, the noise was amazing. There were also bushes and palm trees amongst the cages. It was as if we weren't in the city at all. It was another world which was all ours after closing time. We were able to feed the animals with the caretakers like cuddle the new born gorillas. Mum brought us up on her first commandment 'Thou shalt not commit cruelty to animals'. My family have always had a collection of cats. It was part of life to wake up each morning with a cat on me.

My mother says I have an affinity with animals...

I once had a black cat called Sam, named after an ex-girlfriend, but it ran away.

So much for my affinity with animals. (I think the name was jinxed.)

Me and my cat sharing some Vegemite on toast.

You might remember when 'Rick' dressed up as a surf life-saver for the Australian theme party on *Neighbours*. Well that was my outfit because I used to be a surf life-saver, along with my brothers, at South Melbourne beach. As much as I'd like to sound heroic I can't say I ever confronted a shark or saved anyone's life. The most you'd get patrolling the beach was a syringe in your foot. We'd all be sitting there, zinc on the nose, mirrored glasses, waiting for the next person to step on a bit of glass, or trip over a barrel of nuclear bloody waste from the ships dumping in the bay.

We did heaps of training, got our medallions and became fully fledged surf life-savers. Our team competed in the Australian championships up in Queensland. We raced boats and did the whole bit, but that was as far as it went. I'm nearly due for a refresher course on life-saving skills and first aid.

The view from our Gold Coast apartment.

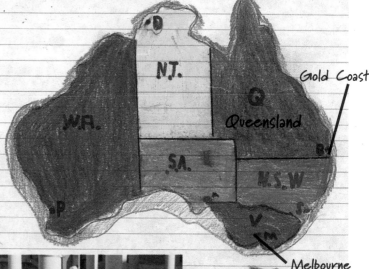

It may be sunny but that water can be cold!

In case you don't know where Queensland and Melbourne are, take a look at this little map I proudly drew when I was six, (Mum likes to keep our school work for posterity's sake.)

I coloured Queensland green because of all the tropical rainforests, but it could also have been coloured red because it's so sunny. The brown Western Australia represents the desert and the yellow Northern Territory is outback.

Schoolwork

I can still remember the day my uncle sat me down and helped me with fractions. Until Grade 5 I never had a problem with school except for maths and science – I was absolutely terrible at them. He sat me down for about half an hour and something just clicked. His method made sense and my maths and science just grew from that time onwards. By the end of year 12 I was getting B+ in physics.

I had always envied anyone in Grade 6 because it was their last year in Primary school. At the award ceremony I watched the smart kids go up and accept their awards. The teachers always left the Dux award for last because that was for the all-round student for that year. This particular student has to be good in all subjects and get along well with students and teachers. When I thought about it, I really didn't have a chance for any of the awards given out. My marks were too low, and I wasn't good at maths and english.

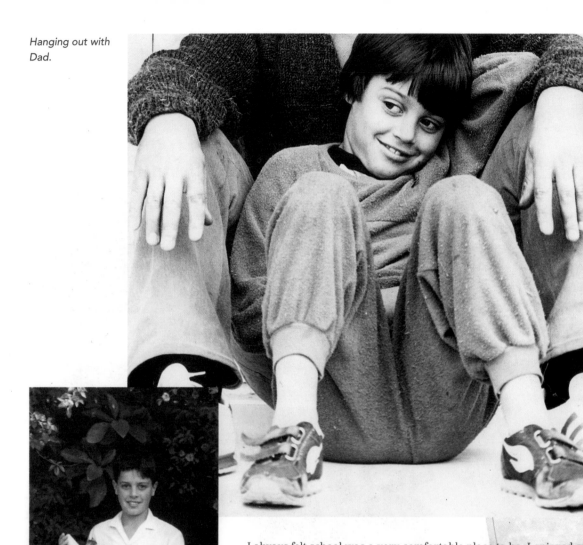

Hanging out with Dad.

I always felt school was a very comfortable place to be. I enjoyed sport, and was captain of my school hockey team. I became captain of my year on the student representative council just to skip class once in a while. But it landed me with all the politics – causing havoc, pushing for more hotdogs and recycling bins around the yard. (I also helped to get green recycling bins put in the *Neighbours* studios.)

Was I in with the 'in' crowd? I was in with 'my' crowd. I didn't sit down and say 'There's the in crowd, I want to be a part of it'. I was never one like that, whatever I did, I was me, that's all there was to it. If people didn't want to be there, check. (Strange – I wondered why I spent a lot of time by myself that year, ha ha.)

Well, I wasn't branded a nerd or anything, I got out of that one because it was the final day of primary school. I just took it with a 'Yeah good, thanks very much', thanks for the bit of paper, what will I do with this? I was amazed that I could do it actually as I had low marks the previous two years.

I guess I could communicate with the teachers because I saw them as just people, having parents who were teachers. They were more like friends. I wouldn't say I

SCHOOL PROJECT: MY LIFE

The awards for the Grade 6s were coming up in a couple of days, before the end of school. I turned up, speculating on who would get what award. The boys and girls went up for their awards and then the big award was next. This award was the Dux of Errol St. When the Principal called out the winner's name and it sounded awfully like mine, I looked around and everyone was staring right at me. I guessed it was me, so I got up and accepted the award.

was the teacher's pet though. I'd give them my fair share of cheek. (It's amazing how a flash of the 'pearly whites' can get your out of trouble.) I must admit in my time I was amongst the kids who made teachers cry. (My sense of humour was never appreciated.)

I'd get kicked out for mucking around. I was always one to imitate the teachers behind their backs. Shining the watch on their bum was always a good one, glue on their seat, whatever I could get away with. I was thrown out of class for being loud and obnoxious on a rare occasion, but all up, I was a good boy (well that's what I wrote on my report).

In the true spirit of the acting profession, I was into Shakespeare from an early age. Those long incomprehensible words just seemed to roll off my tongue. It wasn't the last time I'd tackle them either.

Acting in Macbeth, my first Shakespeare play.

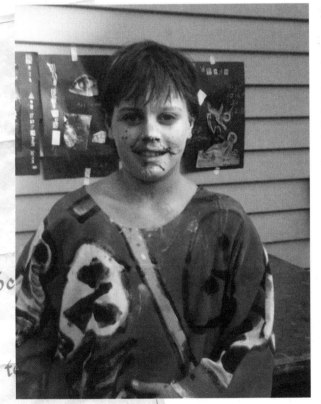

During the year I had been going to rehearsals for the play 'Macbeth' and Phillipa Oriel played Lady Macbeth. After nearly three months of preparation, the performance was ready. Our art teacher, who was producing the play, made the props and designed the clothes. He then got the school children to colour them in. For this play he wanted Phillipa and myself to help him direct the play. Every year Mr Inglebee would put on a Shakespearian play and then the whole school community would come to see it. When the first couple of classes came in to watch, the butterflies in my stomach were jumping around. We had to do the play about four times that day, three during school hours, and one at 5pm. The first time my class performed the play there were lots of mistakes, but as the day went on the play got better and better. The performance we were really looking forward to was the 5pm session. All the parents and teachers were coming to this session, so we were going to make it brilliant. The audience loved it. In my death scene, I couldn't resist taking a big mouthful of fake blood. When the time came, I blurted it out into the air, and stained the roof, and it also went all over me. The play was indeed a great success.

I just had to make the death scene more dramatic. Pity about the roof, but at least it didn't go all over the audience! I like taking people by surprise. Acting Macbeth threw me into the deep end. It was the hook. Acting was for me. I didn't aspire to be a famous actor or to become rich, it was just something for myself really, just to get out there and enjoy what I was doing. It was pure fun and a sense of achieving, having the goal of being somebody else and getting away with it. Delving into another character is quite scary.

My best memories of school were our stage shows. I always had the lead role. We had drama class every two days, we made the sets ourselves, and were involved in all aspects of production. It was just the perfect school to go to. I performed in Carousel at age fourteen . I had an audience of about 3,000 people this time which made me really nervous.

As Othello in my most recent experience of Shakespeare.

When Rick played Othello in the school play, I remembered back to when I had the lead in the school Shakespearian play. It was a laugh playing Othello because I had to wear black makeup all over my face. I didn't have to worry about covering up any black eyes with make-up that day!

Rick had a really bad case of stage fright playing Othello. I must admit, I was quite petrified in my first big role in front of an audience. But, once you're out there and you're into your character, your adrenalin gets you going.

THE INSIDE STORY
JOSIE D'ARBY, BBC CHILDREN'S TV PRESENTER

When Dan came over to England they were running a storyline in *Neighbours* that he was playing a fella who was a black character (Othello). I'm a black person so I pretended when I met him that I was from a black council here in Britain and had come to complain about the fact that he was playing Othello. He was so taken aback it was completely hysterical, he didn't know what to say. He passed me on to his manager telling me he didn't like the storyline either.

What else could I say? I loved that storyline really. It gave me a chance to do some extra comedy and get away with it. You might remember how Rick went off on a tangent because he couldn't remember his lines. 'I hear your voices and they are saying Romeo, lend me your ears, oh curse of marriage, marriage it's a curse, who invented it anyway? Marriage counsellor here we come. Take my life, you get sucked in by some chick then spat out... that's life!' Those words just popped out of my head. I guess I'm a director's nightmare! I just took the mickey out of the whole performance and had the crowd rocking, on my side. It was a lot of fun for Rick and for me!

It was mad that day. I rolled up on the set and was given a new three page script that was all mine. It was hell, all Shakespearian. It wasn't like just giving me three pages to learn in ten minutes. When it's Shakespearian it's like giving me a huge coded numerical thing and trying to remember each different number and letter! Thanks William!

In actuality it was never a big deal learning my lines on the show, even though we had to learn up to twenty-one scripts a week. I'd learn them in bed the night before or read them as I was driving along the highway. (Don't ask me how many accidents I caused.) It was just dialogue in the end, once you know your character it's pretty easy. You just learn your lines, and go, bang, done, no problem.

I can't say I've never stuffed up. One time there was a beautiful girl who came on the show as Aly, the next Elle MacPherson, and I was supposed to invite her to meet me in a room 5B for a talk, but instead another invitation slipped out which, shall we say, was inviting her for a biology class of our own; this particular word replaced 'talk'. A slight Freudian slip . She was nowhere near as embarrassed as I was. We all laughed and hoped to God I didn't say it again. I don't know how it came out, but it just did. Apart from that and swearing, I didn't actually stuff up a great deal.

I improvised quite a bit throughout *Neighbours* and threw in a few lines to lighten up the scene. In a moment of frustration I'd throw in a few 'dohh' which I'm guilty of stealing from the cartoon character Homer Simpson. That became a trademark of Rick too after a while.

There were times where you just had to improvise. Like one day I was in the coffee shop and had a milkshake. I couldn't get my coins out of my pocket to pay, so instead I ended up saying 'Oh yeah, this one's on the house, thanks very much,' and walked off.

What a cute couple!

Kimberley Davies and I were playing Hansel and Gretel in a bar scene once. I remembered the film *European Vacation* with Chevy Chase doing a dance on stage with the yodelling and slapping the arms and face, so Kim and I thought of that and couldn't stop laughing. Here we were slapping each other with these funny hand movements. I'd slap her and she'd slap me back harder until I fell over. None of that was scripted. It made it so much funnier.

Kim and I spent a lot of time together off set. I met Kimberley through Scott many years ago and have remained best of mates ever since. She is one of the most

Dan would make up a lot of humour, even when it wasn't an obviously humorous scene, he'd put his own touch in there. We worked really well together because we both have a very similar sense of humour that we'd add to the scenes. We'd both do mad things that would make the scene that little bit more interesting.

I call him Muttley, that's his name, as in the cartoon character, because he did a stupid laugh one day, you know that hee hee hee, the Muttley laugh and he also looks like a Muttley to me. He calls me Scragger. He came up with that when we were abusing each other one day. We give each other cheek, it's basically about point scoring, and who can be the biggest smartarse!

intelligent and loyal friends that I have.

My friends on the crew and I would conspire to see what we could get away with. The director wouldn't mind half the time (as long as he or she didn't know of course). Sometimes they'd get a bit upset, some were set in their ways, but

He used to like doing crazy little things, like, he'd rehearse doing a line one way and then come the take he'd say it a completely different and funnier way. So on the take you'd be looking at him as your character with a close up on you, your eyes are staring straight through and you're thinking 'You bastard how dare you do that to me?' and he's looking back, knowing he's off shot, going hahaha.

they'd usually end up seeing the funny side at the end of the day (unfortunately when it was too late).

Humour is spontaneity. At its best it's out of the blue. It can only be funny and perfected once. I didn't like when you'd have a laugh doing a scene one way and would have to do it again. I don't see the point of doing it again the same way because you know it's fresh and different, even if it's just rehearsal. You've got to rehearse every scene three or four times before the actual take. I would rather capture that spontaneity back on take and bring up something new.

Funny ideas would pop in my head during the scene. Sometimes the scenes would become so hilarious you'd see the cameras start wobbling, from the camera operators trying to hold themselves back from bursting into laughter. Those scenes were great, then it's cut and we'd all laugh amongst ourselves and then it's all over. I'd always grade my performance on how much the crew

My farewell night.
Left to right:
Kimbo; me; Richie
Rich and Sweet
Raelee.

Peta and I.

were laughing. The crew were my toughest critics. It was nice to be in a comfortable team where they'd say 'Dan that was funny', or 'Dan that was awful, don't do that'.

I sort of cringe when I look back at my early work. There is no class I could have taken anywhere in the world to give me the opportunities *Neighbours* did, and that was working Monday to Friday, acting solidly for at least ten hours a day. And you know something? I loved doing what I was getting paid to do. That, I am thankful for.

After *Neighbours*, if you don't have great skills under your belt there must be something wrong with you – you just pick up so much by constantly acting. Sure you're the same character all the time, but it's your own personal lessons and challenges that develop you as a performer and a person.

THE INSIDE STORY
KAREN NOBLE, STORY EDITOR

Dan was very cheeky on set. He would change lines every now and then. That was something I would always pull him up on. Instead of saying 'nerd' or something like that he'd say 'gumboot'. The scriptwriters would watch the tapes and ask 'Where's this gumboot word coming from?' because we weren't putting it in the script. All of a sudden everyone in the cast was saying it and eventually we tracked it back to Dan because he was saying it the most!

He would make things up, like you'd be doing something and he'd pick up a mop and whack you with it in the middle of the scene, so you've got to accommodate for something that could happen that you didn't rehearse. It was never a problem, I actually like it. It gives you something fresh in the scene, we always used to do it to each other and have a laugh afterwards and kick each other. It makes it more spontaneous and a bit more natural.

Dan and I never used to do many takes at all we used to pretty much get them right first time, he always knew his words or he'd make up his own. He made up lines every day, or on the ends of things, like he says 'dohh', he'd always get that in like if you were having a serious moment or having a fight and he'd come in with 'dohh' now and then and take it in a different direction.

I suggested a few storylines of my own. One day Troy Beckwith (who played Michael Martin) and I were watching the video *Men at Work* and it sparked the idea our characters could get jobs as part-time garbage collectors. In the end Rick started cleaning out bins for a brief while. Unfortunately, my surfing and environmental stories weren't possible due to conflicting story-lines and tight budgets.

Dan did the best pranks, like when it was just coming up to Valentine's Day and a girl had sent him in a pair of panties. He changed the card around and made it to 'My dear Valentine', got rid of any reference to himself, sprayed the pants with fart gas, re-addressed the letter to little Brett Blewett and sent it through the post. Brett opened up his little package, which smelled hideous even though it had been sprayed many days before, but he didn't say anything to anyone. Poor kid. Dan Falzon was definitely respected for that one.

We've got a couple of executives at work and Dan sprayed some of their cushions and the couches with the gas. It was never mentioned, they were far too refined. I don't think the powers-that-be would discuss those sorts of things with the crew, but that odour would have been there for quite some time, but that was so typical of Danny boy.

Above: *The boys of Ramsay Street.*

Right: *Last day on set. Everyone was very supportive.*

SCHOOL PROJECT: MY LIFE

When the summer holidays came we went down to Mount Martha again. Those holidays, we went skin-diving near the rocks, swimming and did some surf skiing. My brothers and I also went to lots of parties. Again we went to Queensland with Mum, by bus. All the places were now familiar.

This time when we got to the Gold Coast, I was very relieved because it had seemed a much longer trip. We stayed at the same place as the year before, because we liked it so much. My brothers and I met up with some of the kids that we had met the year before. Their families had their own apartments in the building.

That year I started up hockey. I really liked playing it. I am extremely fortunate that I have two brothers to play with, because we can go out at any time and practise, instead of having to ring up friends and ask them to come around.

1987 — This year I was in year 7 at University High School. I was put in a class called 7B2. I was told I would be in this class for two years. I met a boy who was in my class called David Allen, and he was a lot like me. He loved the beach, and played the same sports I did.

At the start of the year I was elected to be the Year 7 Brookes representative for the S.R.C. An S.R.C representative is a student who can communicate between the kids and the teachers.

I had a good year at school. I was in the top maths class, because I now found maths really easy. I had many friends as well because my brother had been at Uni High for two years before I came. As Ben was fairly popular, I became Ben's little brother. That was a great year in hockey for me. We had a really great team, because we were all friends. We managed to get in the grand final, against a team of equal strength. At half-time the score was nil all,

1987-88: Hockey

I was tested and became eligible for the gifted children's program that year but chose not to pursue it because, well, those kids were called 'nerds'. Nothing against nerds or anything, but I just didn't like to be separated from my other friends. Uni High was a progressive music and arts orientated school which meant I had more opportunities to act.

The huge grin was from just winning another game.

thanks to some great defending from our team. About ten minutes into the second half, we scored a goal. Then another five minutes later, we scored again. There was three minutes left in the game and I scored the third and last goal for the game. When the whistle went our team were on top of the world. We celebrated with a bottle of champagne and a McDonald's feast.

Dad's a warden at Mount Baw Baw now, so we can go skiing every year. I love the snow — you can have so much fun in it.

SCHOOL PROJECT: MY LIFE

1988 has been a fantastic year for me in hockey. I made the Victorian Hockey team. We toured all around Victoria, playing teams twice our age. We played six games over the week, and won them all. No other team has achieved this honour. The last game we played was against Albury. They had beaten the Western Australian team 3–0. My team worried about this result but the end score tells all. We beat them 8–0.

I am doing quite well in all my subjects this year, but my reading is a bit down, for english. Next week, I will be doing a music exam, maths exam and this 'Diary of my Life' I'm writing will be my english exam.

I ended up getting an A for that project.

There are plenty of hockey fields around the area where we lived in Melbourne so my brothers and I quickly got in on the act, and we took it up to the professional level. I copped a lot of hits in hockey which became quite a regular event to look forward to. Nothing like a bit of a blue to fire up your week.

Sport doesn't have a lot of funding in Australia, so I had scammed sponsorship to pay for my gear and trips. I wrote away to Grays Hockey who make sticks and they helped me out. Mum says 'a little bit of poverty and struggle makes you shrewd'.

I was soon named 'Buster' after a famous Australian hockey player that I had a similar style of play to, and supposedly because he was a 'pretty boy'. I'll leave that one alone I think.

THE INSIDE STORY
BROTHER BEN

At the under-14s camps we used to terrorise the local kids up the road, where they had training squads for the week. We'd run amok in the dark, making noises and throwing waterbombs at the kids. Dan would be in there with firecrackers and his little commando gear hiding in the bushes.

THE INSIDE STORY
MY MATE STUART CAMPBELL

Dan would beat the same player ten times. He has really good stick skills and ball control and hit goals really well. He used to run funny though, kicking his heels up his bum. We used to imitate him doing that.

THE INSIDE STORY
DAD

Danny always had an incredible ambition to succeed. The first sign of that was in hockey – incredible determination – I think it had a lot to do with the separation. They were pretty much on their own when they moved to the city. You learn very quickly moving from a tranquil situation into a city world – they had to learn to be street wise.

Love the headband!

AUSTRALIAN UNDER 15 HOCKEY CHAMPIONSHIPS
HOBART, TASMANIA
1989
VICTORIA — Runners-up

TEAM:
Jason MANOS (C)
Paul BOLTWOOD (VC)
Martin CAMPBELL
Stuart CAMPBELL
Jeffrey CARLAND
Daniel FALZON
Gavin HARVIE
Chris HERRETT

Paul HOOD
Mark JENNINGS
Stuart MAYNE
David MAZZOTTA
Darin MOSS
Andrew PAICE
Dean STRICKLAND
Peter WELLER

COACH: David PURCELL; Asst. Coach: Ross WALKER;
MANAGER: Neil McKAY; Asst. Manager: Andrew CAMPBELL

Right through the ages eleven, twelve and thirteen they were competing in state trials, and they could see the politics of it. If you were 'that' person's son well then straight away you were going to get it. It wasn't just ability. We had no particular background and we were trying to break into this, it was like the stories of people you hear, trying to get on stage and it's not just their ability, it's whether they could even get in the door in the first place and so on. The fact that you've put yourself up against these people and if you don't win or get what you want you've got to cope with that rejection. I've seen Danny rejected when there was every reason in the world he should get into a team. Two days he would be in bed recovering from the disappointment, and the fact that he wanted it so much and it didn't happen. And then after two days he's up again and smiling. So to have that experience when you're young means he's handling what he's doing. That would give him something that maybe other kids didn't have.

If there was money there and there was a hockey trip, it went to that. The money would go on the trip rather than say a vacuum cleaner. You've got only so much money, what do you do? You either feed your kids' hopes and dreams or you have everything perfect in the house, and what for exactly?

AGE 15

In Year 10 at High School I did work experience at a marine centre. It was fantastic. I was in charge of the sea-horse tank, so I was wrapped. I put on a forty-inch wet suit and went searching for marine life under a pier in southern Victoria. It was winter at the time and bloody cold. I went out in a little boat and saw all the sea-lions. My ambition was to be a marine zoologist, and I'd still like to do it. Who knows, maybe I'll direct or produce about it instead.

Don't touch the bottom!

The Big Break

I pursued my craft outside of school and did professional drama classes at St Martin's Theatre. It was there I learned another side to it. Stepping out of the familiarity of school friends and into a group of strangers is where I learned to lose all inhibitions and nervous energy. It made me comfortable acting in a crowded situation.

It wasn't until age fifteen that I thought, 'I'm going to try and make a career out of this'. I knew it was a dodgy business which took a lot of hard work and a lot of luck to get through, so I walked myself into an agency and found myself an agent. A lot of kids ask – how do you get into the biz? You've got to have an agent to get somewhere. I'm one of the lucky stories as far as the TV industry goes. I was working on commercials within a couple of weeks and I was asked to do some modelling courses, which I didn't like. I found modelling plastic.

I wouldn't do it because it's just 'oh look at me'. I didn't have any connection with it. Photo shoots are part of the publicity machine in what I do now, so I do it and it's just part of the business.

After commercials for Nintendo and Toyota I was then on to a mini-series in the role of Paul Kennedy in *Kelly 2*, a children's series, which went to thirty-two countries around the world and was shot on film. I played the role of the main female character's love interest and first kiss. That went for about eight to nine months (the show that is, not the kiss) and then within a month I was going for auditions with *Neighbours*.

So, how did it all start?

Extra!

I was first called in as an extra in *Neighbours* which didn't require an audition. I was to be a soccer player in a scene with Todd (Kristian Schmidt) and Josh (Jeremy Anderson). I had my gear all on, ready to rock and roll and the sun decided not to come out to play. Thanks very much. After hours of waiting around the shoot was called off. Still – got paid. Cool with me. Thinking that was my stint on *Neighbours* and my great contribution to society all over, alas, I was called back weeks later to play a 'fifty worder' as a character called Dylan. A 'fifty worder' is basically the term for an actor who has dialogue not extending over fifty words, Anything over that means you are classified as a guest and the money goes up for your time. As much as I would have liked to ad lib and reach the magic fifty, only having three scripted words made it a little difficult.

The scene was again with Kristian Schmidt, along with Phoebe (Simone Robertson) and the great Maggie Dence (Dorothy Burke, the head mistress). I had the enviable task of putting eight or ten books into a locker with Dorothy hovering over me. This is where it all started. A miracle or fate, you decide. The books I was carrying had to be placed in the locker and once this was done, a shot from a different angle would be taken and then another. It made sense to me that these books for continuity reasons should and must be placed in the same order as in the previous shot. I did this with instinct and only realised later on throughout the years working with extras or 'fifty worders' that most don't understand continuity. I felt it was not only the thing to do but was necessary. I held the scene up by making sure the ten books were in exact order. It may sound very little but knowing *how* makes everyone else's job easier. It benefits not only you, but also the overall standard of a quickly turned over programme like *Neighbours*.

Maggie Dence was the first person I met on the show. This is where the secret came in. Maggie probably doesn't know I realise she passed on a good word to the casting agents and production team about me. I always thought she was a legend anyway.

THE INSIDE STORY
JANE HANCOCK, ASSISTANT DIRECTOR

Danny boy was asked to repeat something, on location where we only have one camera, so you have to do scenes over and over again (from different angles). If you can do them again in the same manner that's fabulous, because that means you have some insight into continuity and what's required to make the scene work – and he did that. He was such a lovely, polite kid. We had some sort of holdup and we were all talking to each other for some time, including Maggie, and he just felt like one of the team from the word go and shortly afterwards he was in.

THE INSIDE STORY
JAN RUSS, CASTING DIRECTOR

It was known that I was looking for a new family at the time and I'd been talking to an actress. She rang later and said, 'about the character you wanted. Have a look at this guy who's playing one of the extras, could be worthwhile.' I do get a lot of calls like that and I don't always take a lot of notice of people, but I'm a fan of this particular actress as well, so that's how it all sort of started. I'd probably have looked at him anyway because I was looking at young guys that age. So I organised for him to come in and do a screen test for me.

There's nothing like playing in the mud!

One week later there was another call from my agent but this time it was for an audition, character unknown. I guess it really didn't hit me, I just went with the flow. I ended up fitting it in straight after hockey practice, so here I was turning up practically covered in dirt, all revved up from a game... and I have to admit, I still felt a butterfly or two.

The Audition

I walked into the foyer dazzled by all the pictures of all the former tenants of Ramsay Street and attempted to fill in a form detailing my weight, height, hair etc. I was lucky to know my eye colour let alone anything else. I figured I was about 5'8", give or take a couple of inches (most likely take) I copied the rest from the guy next to me.

I took a chair, next to about eight other chaps looking remarkably similar to myself. Looking around, some were gazing at their reflections in a glass framed picture. They continually combed their hair, adjusted their clothes and tucked themselves in. It was very catchy. I felt like reaching for my hair as well, but I pulled myself back, thinking of the absurdity of it. To my right was one guy who was not too obsessed with his looks, but he was shaking like he'd seen a bloody ghost, script in one hand and eyes squinted, trying to remember those precious words. Knowing that he should be left alone, I quickly raced up to him and disrupted his train of thought. Oh, the games we play! I stated that the script he had was a lot longer than mine (untrue of course). Boy was he annoyed. Poor.bloke. I offered to do a read with him, whether I'm a good bloke, or because I'm checking out the competition, you decide. After the read, I was the less worried one. Cool. Plan achieved.

I was called in next. I read the part of a young boy and Jan Russ, head of casting for *Neighbours*, read his mother. I was told 'Great, we'll be in touch'. I felt it went pretty well, but you'd say that even if your tooth dropped out during the reading. It's an actor's thing I guess. I walked out ready to face the mob, big grin on my face, a sign of accomplishment, and surprise, surprise, I was met by the others, looking at me with a snarling 'No chance'.

THE INSIDE STORY
JAN RUSS, CASTING DIRECTOR

He came in with that 'Oh hi', that instantly grabs you and you think 'What a nice guy'. I thought yes, he certainly has got charm, and it not only works off camera but it works on camera. That's where the secret lies. Some people can work really well off screen and you think they're terrific but when you see them on the monitor, forget it. It doesn't always work.

I didn't mention the audition to anyone, only my closest family and I went through the whole week waiting for the phone call. I still believe it's bad luck talking about auditions.

I don't like the hype that people make about them. It's like any job interview. Once the job is yours, cool, go for it, but I never classify it as an audition, as much as experience.

With Jan Russ.

The Verdict

Later that week, I was outside playing with the cat when the phone rang. It was my agent. She had the news. Not only did *Neighbours* want to see me again for a final audition but Liz Mulliner, the casting director from *Home and Away* wanted to see me.

Well, I thought, this could indeed be interesting. Still keeping quiet, I secretly went and did both later that week. Again, nervous in both and wow, what an experience!

The chance was now higher. Anything or nothing could happen. A week went by and life went on as normal. I was desperately waiting for the verdict. Then the phone rang. Mum answered and called me inside. 'Dan, it's for you'. It was Linda, my agent. This was it. Do or die.

I grabbed the phone and greeted her with anticipation. 'Congratulations,' she said. My stomach turned over. 'Neighbours would like you to sign up'. I couldn't believe it. I was just about to jump in and speak and she stopped me with 'but...'. 'Hang on, what's up here?' 'Dan, Home and Away want to fly you to Sydney for a screen test with their other contender'. Wow! Now I was in trouble. The decision had to be made *now*. Which show? This was the two top soaps! *Neighbours/Home and Away*, the names spun around in my head. Sorry, but it was all too much for a sixteen-year-old. If I had said yes to *Home and Away* I would have had one contender, and if that fell through it would be goodbye *Neighbours*.

At the time, *Home and Away* was rating extremely well in Australia. The other option was to take *Neighbours*, stay in Melbourne and be a part of something I have always admired. The decision was made. I accepted the position on *Neighbours* and turned down the plane trip to Sydney and the chance to play the character Shane. Yep, that's right, my contender was Mr Dieter Brummer, who is now a very good friend of mine. Oh, it's a strange story I know, but I guess we'll never know how things would have turned out if I'd headed north to Sydney.

THE INSIDE STORY
DIETER BRUMMER
(SHANE, *HOME AND AWAY*)

We're the kind of friends that don't really see each other often, but when we manage to catch up we have a few drinks and a bit of fun. It was hard because Dan used to live in Melbourne and I live in Sydney so a lot of the time we couldn't really ever catch up unless there was a big occasion.

We have a lot in common and our personalities mix well. He's easy to talk to. He's always in for anything.

I received my scripts two weeks later for a character called Marco Alessi, interesting name I thought. I learned my lines, as a good student would and drummed three episodes into my head, only to find out that I was playing the younger brother. That character was none other than Rick Alessi. That character profile read...

THE INSIDE STORY
MUM

When he started on *Neighbours* it was like I was handing him over to another family to take care of him and that was hard.

Rick Alessi is a larrikin and practical joker with a dislike of school. His father, Benito Alessi, had followed the family custom of high academic achievement and presumes one of his sons will follow suit. The burden of this tradition has fallen on Rick. This clashes with his rebellious nature. However, his family is very important to him and he is very loyal and protective of the people he likes and loves.

Rick was fun to play, he bumbled around on screen. He was a scammer but I made him into a bit of a joker as well, a good boy joker that is. I guess the best way to describe him is there was just no malice involved in anything he ever did, he was somebody who everyone could trust . He wasn't the most intelligent kid in the world but he just had a good heart, you don't have to be super intelligent to have a great life, he was uplifting, just a bundle of energy and a lovely person, well that's what I set out to do with him and I hope that's what was achieved.

Rick was my outlet. I could do things with Rick that I couldn't get away with in the real world, there were no limits to his character.

THE INSIDE STORY
KAREN NOBLE, STORY EDITOR

Dan's sense of fun influenced Rick's storylines. We knew we could try anything and he could really pull it off. And there's that sense of cheekiness about Dan that came through as Rick as well. He was always mucking around on the set and he would tease us about the stories we'd given him. He'd come up with completely unreasonable requests, like we should send him away to wonderful countries, things that we couldn't do.

THE INSIDE STORY
RAELEE HILL (SERENDIPITY)

He offered up something completely new and fresh that was unaffected, he wasn't trying to be James Dean, or a sex idol from the sixties, he was just trying to be himself in Rick. He didn't try to assume any look or image, therefore people saw this really comfortable unaffected actor on the screen.

THE INSIDE STORY
TERENCE DONOVAN

Knowing Dan, he has a fairly positive attitude to life, whereas his character was never all that positive, and was a bit of a ditherer, so Dan is entirely different, he knows where he's going.

But then there is a lot of Rick that I'm nothing like.

In time, the scriptwriters pick up on what you're putting into the character and they see what works, so before long you have shaped your own character.

THE INSIDE STORY
RAELEE HILL

Rick was a bit gullible at times. Dan has high energy, but he's not stupid. Dan isn't naive at all, he knows exactly what he wants and he's prepared to put in the hard work to get it. Dan is just a much more mature version of Rick.

Dear Diary

So, how did it all begin? Let me dig out my old diary from 1992. I made sure I kept up my diary when I started on *Neighbours* as it was all new to me. I was learning about the industry and having such a great time, so I'm happy to share it with you.

Let's see here, starting *Neighbours*. It was school and socialising as normal, then, it all began…

HOMEWORK/ASSIGNMENTS SET

MONDAY	not a bad day. Slack as they come came home at lunch time to have a decent lunch cause I was starving. Besides kids at school began asking 20 questions and am slowly getting fed up with it. Wouldn't mind total silence.
TUESDAY	good night. Went for a spin in Jacks sisters car. Jack almost totalled it. But we were never in control. Went to cherry hill and met up with Cam. M, Robyn, Deara and went off to
WEDNESDAY	Woke up bloody early. 1st day on the job Melissa,

That week began with the kids at school asking a thousand and one questions. The word had got around. 'Wow, a star at our school ! What are you going to do on the show?' It's funny how you suddenly become 'special' in others' eyes as soon as you're on TV. I was the same person the week before!

I also met with my tutor who liaised with my school to make sure I was keeping up with my work load. Yep, unlike Rick, I stayed on at school.

The rest of that week was life as normal, went to the movies, homework and went out with the guys on Friday night.

I still recall my first day, driven out there by Mum in the 'yellow esky'.... Here's what I recorded with a few additions in retrospect (my original scribblings are incomprehensible).

29th April 1992 — All hell starts

I arrive first to get make-up on, not one of my favourite tasks, I cringe as it happens. They're telling me that I'll have to get used to it pretty quickly. Then comes the cast photo shoot.

With Felice Arena, who played Marco my screen brother.

That is quick and painless, and I guess with that photo it is cemented. 'Welcome Dan, play your cards right and the town is yours'. Just kidding. So far, it's like an unstoppable train on its way to an unknown destination.

I am the new boy on the block, but I'm quickly adopted by Felice Arena, who plays my older brother Marco. He gives me a comforting smile. We're like two kids clinging to each other on the first day of kindergarten. I didn't know anyone, but needless to say, this time I wasn't screaming! Walking in to any new situation is always scary. I was really nervous about starting to work with all the cast I'd watched on TV, but now I'm one of them.

As the new baby on the show I have been welcomed with open arms. I don't recall names, just their faces. What amazes me about these people is the bond they all have with each other. Everyone seems to huddle together and whisper to each other, no louder than mice. I felt such a strong presence of them all together. I guess that presence comes with respect, and is deserved by none more than Anne Haddy (gran) Alan Dale (Jim),

Stefan Dennis (Paul) and Maggie Dence (Dorothy, the headmistress). The years of work between them have created a bond. And I'm working with them now! WOW!

Afterwards, Kate, the publicist, takes me to Pine Oak Court, better known as Ramsay Street! Travelling from studio down to the street only takes a couple of minutes and those minutes are all Kate's – boy can she talk! If all publicists are like that, I didn't know. She's cool though, which is a good thing, I hear publicists have the control. So we head to the street, pull up at the kerb and are greeted by a security man, who seems half asleep, but I'm sure that is just a special technique to catch wrongdoers off guard. Ha!

I hop out of the car, and look up at the court. WOW. It's certainly amazing. It actually exists! Everything seems a lot smaller. The houses are all there and yes, people really live in them. What a spin out.

We take off after admiring all the doughnut skid marks someone left on the street (probably Scotty Michaelson heading for the surf).

Then it's back to the studio to be greeted by Mum. I say bye to the lovely Kate. 'Welcome to the industry,' she said, and slops a big

At the age of 16, bright eyed and bushy tailed I guess you think like that...

kiss on me. (Welcome to the industry of kisses.) In full view of Mum, oh how embarrassing! With rosy cheeks, I waddle over to mum. We both laugh.

1st Rehearsal

6.30am start. I walked into the green room and there they all were. The first person I found was Scott Michaelson slouched on the couch, still snoozing. It was quite a relaxed atmosphere. Hopefully at this time the actors have learned the scripts sometime on the weekend, if not, a mad scurry commences to hide it from the director.

Natalie caught my eye, she was so stunning. They all had this aura about them.

Scott noticed me and called me over. He whispered to me that he'd just flown in from Adelaide (capital of South Australia) where he had a nightclub appearance, and had had no sleep. Cool. It was my job to keep watch for him.

I liked my screen parents, they kind of took me under their wing. I think I'm going to like working with them.

We went through the scripts and worked out moves, what actors call 'blocking'. I knew my lines and before long I felt right at home. I became mates with Scotty and Felice and we stuck together like mates on their first day at kindy.

Scott was always the busiest out of the whole cast. He would be off every weekend interstate for club appearances or publicity. And during the week was no different. The first

Opposite top:
*The Alessi family,
minus a sister.*

Below: *The sherriff
and his deputy.*

HOMEWORK/ASSIGNMENTS SET

MONDAY	The day went extremely well. I couldn't first taste of rehearsals. I couldn't believe the relaxed atmosphere but still had to know all the lines though. Nat Imbruglia is absolutely gorgeous. Just a babe. End of night I was ~~tired~~ Kelly II called but could fit them in schedule Dae.
TUESDAY	Very early start. (it felt like). Filming day. I was a bit nervous but everything went smoothly. Found out the 'oldies' really aren't that bad. Very nice, talented and interesting people. especially Maggie. Kristian asked me to go scuba diving and I wouldn't mind. Got the day off tommorrow so I will get some work done. P.S. Went for jog.
WEDNESDAY	Great day for getting work done. Contacted all teachers and received work. Most teachers were happy to help which made it easier. However I realised how much work was required. Never mind. It shall be done.
[THURS]DAY	not bad: Acting wise it was quiet emotional and required some real ... wearing a fair ...

time I'd met Scotty was in a nightclub just before I started the show. A best friend of mine, Deano, or as I call him, China, pointed him out to me in a Melbourne club. Not that it is difficult to see Scotty in a crowd, six-foot tall with blonde hair. Anyway, I slowly made my way through the crowd and greeted him. I didn't know what to expect, as people in Scott's position would get people coming up to him all the time. I told him that I was about to start the show and he was wrapped for me. We spoke for hours and got on like a house on fire. From that day onwards Scott and I would become the best of mates and he started calling himself my 'international brother' when he moved to the UK. He had a business mind and thought of more than just the show. He saw *Neighbours* as the base from which numerous, lucrative opportunities would come. This was soon to become my thought also. Scott became my mentor, the man with connections, the man who brought solutions and never problems. *Neighbours* brought that opportunity.

THE INSIDE STORY
SCOTT MICHAELSON (BRAD WILLIS)

For as long as I've known him he's always had a smile on his face. He's superfriendly, doesn't have a bad word to say about anyone. He was one of the people I liked working with the most on my time on *Neighbours*. We were always having a laugh.

As a mate, he's a honest, genuine kind of guy, I've got a lot of time for him. I looked out for him like a younger brother, I'm six years older than him, but he's an intelligent guy, he doesn't miss much. He's been really enterprising. He figured out a good way to go, he doesn't wait for the phone to ring, he gets off his bum and tries to make things happen. You can go a long way with that kind of attitude.

Its huge audience could make us actors/businessmen. It was Scott's philosophy, not mine. Even during those early days I could see the sense in it. Not only to take it to the limits and create further opportunities, but in this business you take on a role that could last only half a year and then you'd be looking for another acting role to survive and pay the bills. We had to look after ourselves.

Tuesday 5th May 1992

I woke up raring to go. Here was my chance to put yesterday's rehearsals into action. I had to be on set at 6.45am. I was very nervous, it was my first real day of shooting, but I had a job to do and I just did it. In my first scene Rick got expelled from boarding school for putting the Principal's nickers on the flag pole and was back in Ramsay Street to see Mum and brother Marco and explain everything. So he turned up on the doorstep and said to the folks 'I'm not going back to school...'

Very early start. (it felt like). Filming day. I was a bit nervous but everything went smoothly. Found out the 'oldies' really aren't that bad. Very nice, talented and interesting people especially Maggie. Kristian asked me to go scuba diving and I wouldn't mind. Got the day off tommorow so will get some work done. P.S. about for joy.

The scene immediately established my character as a rebel.

Like my diary says, I was nervous, but it went well. My screen parents (Elspeth Valentine and George Spartells) helped me through the scene, but I didn't feel an amateur working with professionals for long. I had become part of the family.

Wednesday 6th May

I went to school as normal but realised the huge workload I was about to endeavour on top of a full-time job.

Great day for getting work done. Contacted all teachers and received work. Most teachers were happy to help which made it easier. However I realised how much work was required. Never mind. It shall be done.

Handwritten note (top left)

not bad: Acting wise it was quit
emotional and required some real
acting. Melissa was wearing a fair
number. People from tourist trips
watched the filming. Amazing stuff as
I am at Jacks now for training.

Thursday 7th May

It was funny that day how tourists turned up by the bus-load – this was not just any Melbourne suburban street, it was a chance to see the famous Ramsay Street not through a TV tube!

11–17th May

That week, as you can see, was school, *Neighbours*, school and more *Neighbours*. Life was full on, staying up to 4am doing homework, and then up for 6.30am starts on set. I'd go to school for an hour class and then race back to studio. It was living on adrenalin, and I loved every minute of it.

On Friday I wrote about learning how a sense of humour makes people remember you. I always try and have a laugh out of every situation.

WORK/ASSIGNMENTS SET (handwritten)

to school first – then Channel
then school – then chanel
then home. What a day
was getting confused. Just
seld which went fire.

off from filming so I had
lot of time to spend at school
catch up on work. I have
ed out on. Didn't go to training
had a lot of work to do.
up to 4.am.

location and rehersals. Had
mos for half of the day
the rest I was trying to get
done. Met some of the cast for
ool cast. Some of them one up them
it Wonkers. Saw Katrina Macean + Rob Bail.
up to 4am doing Hwork
up I was however marched
All day at a deserted building
for filming. It was good for.
pecially as it rained. Say Nat again,
I don't know. Mox + Micheal Garcia
on Kelly II was also there. Finished cart
Finished all my due English + R+D
minutes before bell. After filming
was however on the
home, I learned something.
you have a sense of humour people
remember you and like you. it also makes
you feel great.

rent/Teacher): _____

A Time of thinking. Just watched the
amazing story of Anthony Hopkins. An
actor (a real one) made me feel like the
slag off a opscrap iron. But hey, you've got to
start somewhere. Another point where the do I belong,
don't even feel others are and feel the same way I do.

THE INSIDE STORY
MY MATE DEAN STRICKLAND

He's the biggest scammer and prankster you'll ever know. At the cinema we used to go inside and he'd ask people for their ticket, saying he'd lost his and he'd get about three or four different tickets and get all his mates in for nothing. Come to money, he'll scam everything.

THE INSIDE STORY – MUM

Danny's laugh is what I'd say his friends love about him, and that's what I love about him too. He loves to throw his head back and laugh. It's not a sarcastic laugh, it's just a laugh. I think that's what is his centredness, his sanity, is that he can laugh at it all, and be a terrible cynic. This family is very cynical, most Australians are very dry and cynical. Just the ability to rip things apart and laugh at them.

Monday 18th May

I admire Anthony Hopkins as an actor and a talent although I classify myself as an apprentice. It can be difficult to be taken as a serious actor when many people look down upon soaps as not real acting. But soaps, unlike films which take years of preparation, are turned over at the rate of two and a half hours of television a week, working up to fourteen hours a day to produce it. This means there is just not time to spend on rehearsals and film extra takes. Every movement in television is scripted and directed like a puppetry situation – we know every point to walk, turn, where the camera is staring in our face for close up, and every word has a cue for where to move next.

There is not a great deal of production in Australia, due to limited funds. For many aspiring actors *Neighbours* provides a brilliant break, and keeps very talented actors in work, as well as the crew. How can that be knocked?

That day I also wrote about not fitting in. It can be hard because as soon as you're on tellie you're separated and treated differently. The kids at school could not relate anymore, they thought I'd changed. I hadn't changed personally, only my lifestyle had.

Tuesday 19th May

The loneliness is a bit like a prison, people only want to come up to you and say G'day because they sort of know you and your face is plastered on magazines everywhere! You start missing the people who want to know you for you. So it's such a relief when you're back with family and friends who have always known you.

Everyone in the business senses it. You start running out of people who you can turn to and that's the end of the line for a lot of actors. They start feeling it and then they work out they're by themselves. That's the loneliness.

It's even worse for the actors who move to Sydney from the other side of the country. They're suddenly under immense pressure and don't have the familiarity and support of their loved ones. They have to cope alone, with everyone pulling at them. You're suddenly a teenager with adult responsibilities, like contracts to think about.

When I'm in England I still call my mother about once a week. I call my Dad about once a fortnight but as soon as I'm home I'm straight down to Mount Martha to see him and we muck around there. I still haven't worked it out whether I'm lucky, but I have a lot of people I can ring up who I can talk to so I'm not alone. I'm at the stage where I'll fly someone over for Christmas just to keep a little sane. And at the end of the day, I realise that to do what I love involves some sacrifice, which means enduring long periods away from home.

It can be hard, but I've got my good mates who I can turn to. I can speak openly with Scotty, Alex or Kimbo – it really just depends who my next phone call is to. Then there's Raelee Hill. She's like my sister, she's such a beautiful girl. Richard Grieve is another great mate. I've never met someone who can tell a story like he does. He's too cool for his own good.

The dream team.

All of us can just pick up the phone anytime, we have that luxury together so it is really nice. We just clicked straight away. We've all have such good times together.

Then there are my mates who I have known for what seems like all my life; closest are Deano and Stu (Mojo) – alias the 'Frog Brothers'; then there's Jason (Jack), Brett, Thommo, Jeremy, Mark, Carson and Softie. You can never have enough brothers!

Quite an easy day, however it was very tiring. Did score, watched by Pommi tourists: felt bad because I didn't talk to them before I left. Spoke to Nat for a while, talking about loneliness and stuff. Went for run + sprints and watched Vic 21 vs Malaysia. Too tired for homework – going to bed.

I guess I started to talk to my diary like it was a real person listening, in a way it was – a constant companion to always be there, who knew me intimately. Sometimes when I'm on the road, away from the people who are close to me, I'll jot down what's happening and write lyrics as well. It's the easiest way to work things out when you have time alone.

> Rehersals at ch:10. Did work on English between brakes. Finnished at 6:30 pm. Went to Felices with him + Tutor (Math). Went to Pizza Hut for 5 buck deal. Not bad.

Thursday 21st May

Ah yes, the Young Ones and Black Adder. After a day's work it was so relaxing to come home and sit in front of two of my favourite shows. Little did anyone know I'd stolen a bit of Rick from Rik Mayall's character in *The Young Ones* for my character.

> Very eerly morning start. Stged at Felices as it was eorly. Did location for 10 hours out in Boronia. All went well exept very tired. Bonus was that I got to meet Tiffany Lamb. (Not Bad). Went to bed fairly late due to English essay due, which I didnt finnish because the Young Ones + Black Adder was on.

I also nicked a bit from Kirk in the American sitcom *Growing Pains*. He was the nice guy, still a good bloke, everyone felt a bit sorry for him because he played the dumb bloke and I guess that's what Rick was originally. He worked into more of the entrepreneurial side, but at school he was just never smart and I guess a lot of people related to that. Not everyone is cut out for school, but at the same time it doesn't mean you're no help to society, you're still a part of it all and he carried a smile around everywhere he went.

Then there was Bart from *The Simpsons*. I was a fan at the time. Cartoons are fantastic in the way that you have to watch them several times, particularly *The Simpsons*, because things are happening all the time. When you watch it over you see things you didn't catch the first time. I remember watching an episode a third time, and suddenly I saw this little mouse and the Simpsons running around at the floor, it bumped into a seat, got knocked out for a second and then took off.

Above: My best mates. Left to right: Dean; Mark; Stu; me; Brett; Jeremy; Jason.

You'd never see that first and that's where I guess my upstaging began, always trying to do something in the background.

Even when I wasn't on camera the majority of the time, particularly in the first two and a half years, I was always doing something or breaking something in the back of the shot and then just fixing it quietly. Like, 'oops, I hope Mr Willis didn't see this', and scratching stuff and saying little comments, yeah that was all me, that was where it all came from. The crew knew all about my tactics in every scene, they'd think 'here we go again'.

Friday 22nd May

Another early start. Filming at Studio today so wasn't to bad. Tutor cracked because I did homework in publicity office

Naughty boy that I was, I did my homework in the publicity office. I was meant to only study in the designated classroom... But Cath my tutor was cool. I started calling her 'Special K'. She got a kick out of that, it started her day off with a lift (her nickname, not the cereal).

Wednesday 27th May

Ah ha, what do we have here? First TV Week Appearance today. My picture with brother Felice and parents. So, is that supposed to mean I'm a star now?

Got up pretty early. Did exam and I've got No idea how I went. Went to work and did 9 scenes. Wo!!. Seem to go pretty well. Stayed up to 2:30 am getting work done. First T.V week appearence

At first the pressure of juggling publicity on top of school, work, and hockey was turning me into a mess. It took a good two years to realise I had to start saying no. Mum was always saying to give up hockey, but I loved that too much. Withstanding pressure makes you a stronger person. I've always grown up just wanting to be better. It doesn't necessarily mean money or living in a greater house, just being a better person. Success to me is being a better person. Whether you're living in a tent in the hills or a mansion in the city it's all about being a better man.

I was sick right throughout 1992 with colds, flus, sore throats, lack of sleep, constantly battling with myself to stay fit, but I just kept thinking, 'Come on man, you've come this far, don't stop now', so I haven't and I just keep going. You can't take sickies when there's a show to run.

PRESSURE

At my school, just finding your seat was always harder than the exams. I was always the last one to find my name because it was all numerically coded, probably logical, but Tom and I couldn't work out what the caper was.

Tom and I did well in our exams in the end and we made it to University, but found we couldn't conform to Uni life.

I applied a couple of months before my exams for Rick to be written out of the storyline for just that week. They had to have a lot of notice because storylines are written three to four months ahead. Then there is six to eight weeks' time span between recording and when the show goes to air.

Grundy's were very accommodating about our schooling, like with our own

tutor and portable classroom, and they always had a copy of our school schedules to try and slot our scenes in with our classes.

Monday 1st June

Today was a laugh. Scott, Terence Donovan and I just got the giggles. It was Todd's funeral scenes.

HOMEWORK/ASSIGNMENTS SET	
MONDAY	Another bloody early start and Filmed funeral scenes for Todd (Kristian Schmid). I had the most Hilarious day with Scotty Michaelson and Terence Donovan. Laugh so much it hurt. Work dan well at funeral. Got here eventually but was exhausted as usual

I don't know what it was, I guess being surrounded by death does funny things to you. In the end we were told by the director to hide behind the rest of the cast. Oops, in trouble. And Terry was terrible, Terry Donovan, just sits there and doesn't help you stop, he's laying in the jokes too.

Terence Donovan and I play off each other's jokes. Meeting up with him has been like, wow! To think years ago I was watching Jason, his son, and now I'm privileged to be working with his dad. Cool. 'Tez' (as I'm now calling him) and I are becoming close friends. He is such a generous man, so open and willing to tell of his experience. He sees I respect him and he gives me his time and the wisdom that he's encountered over the years. He's the sort of man that you sit down and listen to every word he says, 'cause if you don't you're going to lose something.

He's been like a father on set, whenever there's a problem, he'll sit the other guys and me down and explain it all to us.

He's telling me to slow down, because I have to control my energy, I tend to get hyper and he says I want to get all my lines out too quickly. I'm learning I throw my arms around too much and have to calm my body language down. Anything on TV gets magnified ten times, it's not like stage where you emphasise every movement. On camera it's seen close up, every expression, every eye movement, it's there on the screen.

Terry and I still catch up all the time. 'How you going Dick' he says (must be something to do with rhyming with Rick). He gives me a big bear hug when we say seeya later.

Look Mum, I'm on TV

Six weeks after my first acting scene my work had been edited and was ready to go on air. Here's what I had to say about the day I hit the screen, big time.

THE INSIDE STORY
TERENCE DONOVAN

I send him up and call him the Maltese Falcon, but he's like a son to me and we have good fun together, we always have a laugh. We became good friends. He's very bright and intelligent and has an engaging personality.

One thing I found about Dan Falzon which I greatly admire, was he was doing his schooling. So many of the kids got into the show and didn't continue. Dan did and passed. He wasn't seduced by the business as so many young ones have been. He hasn't allowed success to get in the way of exercising his brain and intelligence to the fullest degree and I admire him for it.

The time had to come. I was on. Tonight Dad came down from Mount Martha and the whole family watched me on the tellie. Well, they did. I couldn't face it. I hid behind the couch. I couldn't stand to watch my family's faces as they saw me appear. I was scared of their reaction. What did they think of me, and of my acting? In Kelly, I had just played myself really, the character wasn't so defined. This time, I was up there as one of the main characters, during mainstream viewing, for the whole world to see! They all laughed. Dad goes 'what the hell are you doing? What's this acting caper?' I had no answers for him, I was still buried behind the cushion.

My eyes peeped up occasionally, cringing, 'Is it over yet?' but it was strange.

I was anxious to see what my family thought of this 'other life', but they were supportive and just laughed with surprise. Not watching myself became the norm. Once I do a scene, that's it, I've lived it for that moment, I don't look back. It's on to the next scene.

Funnily enough, many people think being on *Neighbours* means you've 'made it' or you're special because you're 'up there'. That is losing sight of what it's all about, actors work for the love of it, for performing, the thrill is delivering the performance, not all the accolades in being a 'somebody'. Journalists have asked me questions along the lines of 'Well now that you're a somebody...' I'm like 'I've been a somebody for twenty years already thanks very much'.

THE INSIDE STORY
DAD

It was funny for the family seeing him on the TV in a different way. How was he going to come across? From being the hockey player, everyday kid and all of a sudden he's on the idiot box. I thought it would be quite humorous, but it was overwhelming to see someone you live with all of a sudden in there, playing a role in a different family scenario.

| TUESDAY | Got up a 6:00am, picked up 7:30 (Great). Went to Gunnamatta did beach scenes with Scotty + Natalie and it was cool. Had to suck face with Nat but she was cool about it and I wasn't saying no (cheeky bastard) Headed off to Pin Oak to a scene which got cancelled and then off to studio for one scene which went well. Home at last and feeling very tired and exhausted. Studied and then to bed. |
| WEDNESDAY | |

Tuesday 9th June

Just another day 'Sucking face with Nat', yep, my dream come true. Kissing scenes can be quite embarrassing, but when you're friends you just have a giggle about it afterwards.

Thursday and Friday of that week were a mad rush to get my English essays done on time – staying up to 3am writing, and handing it in just in time on Friday. You might be thinking why stay on at school when I had become an actor? Well, being lucky enough to be cast on *Neighbours* is not the pinnacle, it's just the beginning. Jan Russ, the casting director always told me, *Neighbours* is an apprenticeship, like any other job. You learn the craft for about three years first, but with acting, you never stop learning. You keep going for another challenge, to grow as a performer.

School was something I couldn't envisage as unfinished, I was always planning on going to Uni to study marine biology to be a marine zoologist. You never know how long your role will last so I kept on with my studies, as difficult as it was fitting it in.

oors. then went back
Absolutely loved life.

As I was feeling pressured with school work on top of *Neighbours* and hockey, Rick was also finding school too much. He had taken on looking after the coffee shop as well as triathalons, the school play, you name it. This was just one way my life was mirroring his. I didn't know what was going on any more!

When Rick jumped out of the plane to conquer his fear of heights, I too was jumping out with a parachute in Adelaide, South Australia. It was a stunt as a presenter for a pilot (a pilot is an example episode of a new show). That was just the maddest experience, falling down at speed that gets your adrenalin going overtime. Everything just clams up when you're ready to drop, then you just go for it. I'd recommend it to anyone.

I didn't actually jump for that scene, it was all filmed on the ground. The producers, Grundys, wouldn't let me because of the conditions of my insurance. I don't know how much we were all worth, but it was a lot of money once we were under contract. Luckily, I was able to do the real thing a few weeks later anyway.

I rang Dad while I was in Adelaide after I'd just fallen. He spun out. I told Mum once I was back in Melbourne, I thought she'd worry. So a week later I put the tape on and said 'Hey Mum, take a look at this'. That caught her by surprise.

THE INSIDE STORY
MUM

I remember at one stage when he was into *Neighbours* he made some comment and it was 'I really love my life,' and he really meant it. He loved his life. It was not like in a conceited way, it was 'Wow, this is mindblowing' and I think that's how he approaches a lot of his life. I thought isn't it fabulous to be able to say that, because I don't know if I ever have.

I often have bursts of poetry that come into my mind...

Cradle is still warm, and
no harm is being alone.
What a nervous world. Betrail is
tragedy and
failing is the success of some.

3 August: Bang — you're dead!

Today I discovered that one of my greatest mentors, Maggie Dence, the first cast member I met, was leaving. Then I was told about Felice going as well. I couldn't believe it. That was my first taste of the reality of the business. Some very dear friends just 'Seeya later', bang! From that day I realised just how insecure the industry is and what actors have to live with – that scary thought, waiting for the script where you die horribly or you're written out of the show by moving out of Ramsay Street! Everyone can be replaced, that's just the blunt truth of it all, and no one should ever feel like they're secure. I hoped that one day I would leave of my own accord without being asked to leave.

Shortly after, Scotty was moving on to further his career as a producer so I was left to fend for myself.

The writers told me there was so much they could do with Rick, which was lucky. Whereas others get written out because they can't think of anything else to do with them, Rick had a scam a week!

I felt really bad for my mate Felice. All I could think was, one door closes and another opens, that's the only way to look at it, but, you've got to open the door yourself. Felice is a funny fellow and extremely talented. He'll be fine.

HOMEWORK/ASSIGNMENTS SET	
MONDAY	Early day of week. Got told about Maggie Dence leaving. Felt devestated. However life has to goo on I suppose. I well still pissed off. Went to school that morning
TUESDAY	What a day of events. The family was going well then Whammo Felice gets the arse and so did young Ben gutcross. Mate I was losing the plot something shocking. Went to training and did alright I suppose. Night
WEDNESDAY	Rehersals + Studio. Still getting over the shock of the sackings. Worked out trip to England with Margaret. Whoppee. Finished late then went straight to bed. Night

Who's Bad?

For weeks I had pushed my luck and hassled the scriptwriters to give Rick some sort of adventure, like a trip to see the whales in Antarctica. Then one day I thought they were getting me back with a joke about sending me to London. But an airline ticket was flashed in front of my face. Yep, they were for real. Rick and Debbie were going to win tickets to the Michael Jackson concert in London. I couldn't believe it. At sixteen, it was incredible! I had never been overseas before!

Monday 17th August 7.30pm Australian time

Awesome. What a sight. A sunset illuminates the sky somewhere near Darwin, the top end of Australia, and we're heading for Bangkok.

Miles of undisturbed outback and wildlife life lie below. Just like the desert in the west we crossed on our way to Perth when I was a child. I will never forget the isolation and stillness of that land. Unbearable heat and just raw wilderness. Such another world, no barriers – just freedom.

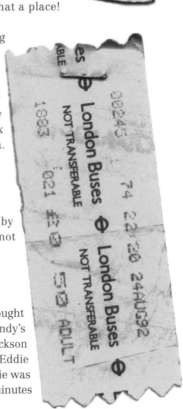

12am Australian time

Bangkok. What a strange place. Feeling like a zombie.

12am – 3pm

Wow! Thirteen hours. Half-sleeping, half-eating, bones aching, vision blurred. But that's cool. Arrived in England finally at 3pm Australian time, 6am Tuesday morning English time. Didn't sleep, we had to stay awake so jet lag didn't catch up. Met up with our chaperone Steve and driver Ashley. Taken to the hotel and *wow* what a place! Kingsize bed, spa, stereo, cable TV... who needs a backyard any more?

Our chaperone took us around the streets of London. What an amazing place. The streets are chaotic. Looks like it's quicker to walk anywhere than to drive. Great variety of shopping, but very expensive. Called up Mum back home, she was amazed that I have a room like I do all to myself. Then went to the gymnasium. Great weights room. Apparently Anthony Hopkins works out there. As you pump weight you get a brilliant view outside of the ninth floor. You can see millions of the old-fashioned black cabs. Spent dinner at Hard Rock Cafe, loved all the original memorabilia. Burgers worth $18 Australian.

Wednesday 19th August

Had a BBC publicity shoot which went on for ages, then went shopping by myself in Oxford Street after a workout in the gym. Sunnies disguise is not working. Got stopped for autographs so couldn't get much shopping done.

Thursday 20th August

Filming today. Had my £35 ($70 Australian) breakfast, then off to shop. Bought a pair of shorts and a NFL jacket for £50. They're pretty cool. Then to Grundy's production office before heading off to Wembley Stadium for the Michael Jackson concert. We were issued with special passes and met a cool man named Eddie who is Michael Jackson's main man when he's in town. Accompanying Eddie was a stunning lady about six-foot tall with long blonde hair. We had twenty minutes

to do four camera shots with no rehearsals and beat the crowds pushing to enter the stadium. Phew, got it done in time. Eddie took Marnie and I on to the stage before it started. We looked out at the huge crowd just sitting and waiting there. I totally spun out... What a sight.

Went to the back of the stadium to get some shots with a bunch of kids, then the camera got too close to the stage and a couple of big dudes came and confiscated the camera. We were suddenly kicked out of the Jackson concert, left outside wondering what was going on. We got the tapes back but the Jackson crew wanted to see what we had filmed. Anyway, we eventually were given some tickets and Marnie, Steve and myself got in. Michael Jackson was fantastic. What a performer. Every move he made was perfect. What a talent. He possesses such power and elegance. What a total spin out. He put so much into it. It was like everyone united. Imagine having that many people transfixed by your performance.

Above: *Like the hat dude!*

Friday 21st August

Early start. Filmed all day at Trafalgar Square with crowds of people swarming around us, especially because the scene involved a camera being stolen. Did the same scene in all different places – in cabs, double decker buses, on buildings, bloody everywhere!

Saturday 22nd August

Another early start. Fourteen-hour working day full of about eight scenes. Filmed in two locations – an average English suburb... and Arsenal football club. When it was all over I phoned a nightclub called The Limelight and organised getting in. Went with Marnie, James (camera assistant) and Jeremy (cameraman) and his wife Sara. Got to the club about 1am. I got them all in and into the VIP room. Thank you very much. No such thing I'm afraid. The four of them ended up leaving me by myself. But I thought, 'oh well' because I met up with a very attractive Liverpudlian whose accent I just loved. She has the most stunning figure. She's twenty-one and works in fashion designing. Her name is Tracey and she's beautiful. We didn't do anything together, but talked a lot. I slipped her a quick kiss then I wasn't sure what was next. We mucked around till 3am. Her friend drove me back to my hotel and that was the end of a very interesting night. I hope to see her again, but that is unlikely. Oh well.

Sunday 23rd August

Woken up by a phone call by Stevo, which was OK because I wasn't going to be slack. Fortunately I didn't have a hangover. Couldn't be bothered going to the gym though. Headed off to a market and bought Doc Martins. Then went to Hampton Court Palace where King Henry VIII lived in the 16th century. Wow what a place, huge and amazingly beautiful. We left after completing the maze good old Henry set up. On the way home we passed a castle the Queen Mother sometimes lives in. It's huge and looks like a castle from hell. Took up a whole hill top.

Monday 24th August

After a long day filming the montage of London we went to a Spanish nightclub. Then we hit another bar, can't remember the name. Drank vodka and orange. Awesome. We couldn't be bothered hanging around. It rained down on my new white jeans. Passed some drunken Australians causing havoc. Glad to get to bed, thought about Tracey for a little.

Tuesday 25th August

Said goodbyes and boarded the plane again. Felt good to be going home. We passed Czechoslovakia, Romania, Singapore, Sydney and then finally home. Marnie and I got into the limousine and went home sweet home.

It was the most fantastically awesome, outrageous experience of a lifetime, all time, totally magical and cool trip of this era. And the best thing was, it went very slow. Britain – I'll be back.

BOARDING PASS

NAME OF PASSENGER
FALZON/D MR
CLUB WORLD
LONDON   LHR
TO
MELBOURNE   MEL

FLIGHT   CLASS DATE   TIME
BA 0011 J 25AUG 1400

GATE   BOARDING TIME   SEAT   SMOKE
5   1320   23D

PCS   WT   UNCKD   BAGGAGE ID NUMBER   CK
1   DOCUMENT NUMBER

Tuesday 15th September

I really dressed up today. We're shooting a dress-up day at Erinsborough High next week and I couldn't handle Rick wearing a boring 'normal' outfit that they'd shown me, so I went straight to wardrobe and found something much more daring – a panda bear suit. I was bouncing around in it, trying it out for size. Scared some of the cast, but they knew who was underneath! Nothing like a good old bear hug.

Looks like I'll be hot in that suit next week under the hot lights.

HOMEWORK/ASSIGNMENTS SET

MONDAY	Hey how's my favourite Diary. Monday. Up at 6:30 and off to work. Just a short day however at work, I was then off to school to do Chemistry pracs. Yep then I had a beautiful sleep and got docked up for speech at Mums work. Turned out I didn't get through speech but wasn't necessary. Signed a few things and that was that.
TUESDAY	4 scenes out at location to start the day. I was wearing my bear suit. Cool man. Anyway I'll be hot next week in studio. Speaking of that I was off to film 5 scenes in school room. Went well. Went home, Went out with the boys from school to the Clyde. Walked home.
WEDNESDAY	Day off from work. Yeeah, Yeah. Get up at 11:00 am, slack ass, Went to Drivers to edit video (communication project). Half done, then went to Borthangs, to finish of 4 Pracs to right up before Friday. Anyway got them done + also finished editing. Went home did homework + slept.

It was like, if I'm going to dress up, I wanted to do it big time. Rick was the ring leader at that stage, every prank, everything that went wrong in the school was blamed on Rick, you know, he was the real joker. So I felt that he had to stand out.

The wardrobe department used to suggest Rick's clothing to me and we would come to a compromise. I suggested loud colours and big designs normally with a big fit, that way I felt like a real galah. Personally, I like dark colours and tighter clothing. My favourite outfit would have to be just a pair of Levis and a T-shirt. I buy most of my clothes at opp shops, I can't relax in brand new clothes. I like them dodgy. I also wear a lot of rings and chockers which mainly came from fans actually. I also have a turquoise ring which has sentimental value to me.

Thursday 17th September

Went to school after shooting a few scenes in the morning, thought I was finished for the day, but they called me out for another scene when I was in class. My mobile phone went off right in the middle of a test, how embarrassing!

The mobile phone was for convenience sake – and sometimes for a laugh. My former driver, who used to pick me up in the mornings when I wasn't driving, won't let me forget how I used to see a car in front of us with a business sign on the back of the vehicle and I'd call up the mobile number. This was while he was driving so it was so funny to see him panic, trying to find his phone amongst the tools or whatever at the same time as holding the wheel. He didn't want to lose the call and lose business, but just as he'd have it in his hand, I'd hang up. Very naughty, I know, but good for a laugh.

> FRIDAY Started off day being picked up by a special driver for commercial. Went to weights place. All stuff was shot with me doing weights in the dark light. Went well apparently but I was knackered. Got to work and had to organise the word process for Julie Mullins off ... it almost drove me bonkers.
>
> COMMENTS (Parent/Teacher):

Friday 18th September

Today I had to shoot a commercial for Channel 10 to advertise Neighbours. *They filmed me pumping iron at the gym. It's going to have a couple of girls discussing 'What's hot?' and then they're going to show me, filmed in black and white, apparently looking sexy (good luck), lifting weights with a close-up shot on my muscles. They were happy with it in the end, but by the time the lighting was OK and heaps of takes later, my muscles were about to collapse!*

I didn't start out to be a pin-up boy. Rick was a regular school kid for one and a half years. Looks weren't important. I didn't have to look 'cool'. It wasn't until the last couple of years that my image changed. You start being put up into the spotlight, like with the muscle man advert and take things a bit more seriously, your hair gets a bit shorter suddenly, sideys come off, you're at the gym a bit more, and you grow up I guess.

Friday 30th October

> FRIDAY Up at 8.00. dressed for war. Bought eggs and the fight was on. We all ... up each other with bombing. It was great. I was covered head to toe with eggs, water, flour + food. Pissed down rain. But it was worth it. I worked out I really like my year 12 mates, and now
>
> COMMENTS (Parent/Teacher): we have to separate.

Well, that pretty much sums up the last day at school – egg and flour fights, running amok and getting away with it. That's kind of a tradition in Australia; don't know about you but Aussies just take vengeance on all the teachers we dislike, letting down their tyres and wrapping cars in toilet paper.

Monday 2nd November – Fame

'The sunny and hat still don't work' I wrote. The things we do to disguise ourselves! I've never gone to the extreme of a wig. Perhaps I should try one of those plastic noses with the fluffy hair down the sides. No, that wouldn't work – everyone would really know it's me. It's the kind of prank Rick would get up to.

Most people approach me as Rick. One time a lady came up and told me off for sleeping around, I don't know what she was on, because Rick never slept around anyway. I just laughed at her. She said 'If you were my boy I'd put you on my knee and give you a good hiding'. I just replied: 'Thanks sweetheart, but wait until you're asked!' She was about ninety years old too. I've had busloads of grandmothers grab me and plant big sloppy kisses on my cheek, there's like forty grannies going insane, but you can't say no to the old dears. You can tell off the kids for being silly but you can't do that to their grandparents. I call them the Grey Brigade.

I've holidayed in countries like Spain, Italy, Canada, America and still been approached by fans. Whichever neighbourhood I'm in, I'm still recognised as a neighbour. A lot of actors have difficulty with the constant recognition.

Many fans assume you don't have anything else to deal with in your life, but we all pay our bills, have difficulties in our personal lives, go to work, just like anyone else. The only difference is people are watching all the time. But that's why we act, we act for an audience, so we do respect our fans. But it does often mean you can't just run into a shop for five minutes because you suddenly have a line of people waiting to talk to you. Actors need to be in good spirits constantly. It's a twenty-four hour job. You finish work for the day, but the moment you pull into a petrol station, you're reminded of your job! It's not just a matter of coming home and switching off from work. To be an actor you certainly require tolerance in coping with the demands put on you.

THE INSIDE STORY
MUM

Dan would never be unpleasant to anyone. He has people coming up to him all the time, they're pulling at him and you can see he's just depleted, because he's the sort of person that's eaten alive.

Mum taught students who couldn't comprehend how I could be her son because I lived on Ramsay Street. No matter what she said to convince them, they couldn't separate fiction from reality.

I lived near a girls' school and they'd follow me. In the end, there was no way of keeping my address from them. One time they tortured me by singing the *Neighbours* theme tune outside my window so I would eventually come out, but I was inside, as tired as ever and like a baby being sung to sleep.

Fans are cool, nothing dangerous. You can see them a mile away, in the rear-view mirror as you're driving along. It's no problem, if it was I'd be in the wrong business. Some actors sit there and whinge about too much work and attention, but my motto is 'Just deal with it'. Casting director, Jan Russ was always telling all the others 'remember you're in people's living homes day and night, you're their friends'. At the end of the day fans are the ones who make or break you.

People love to have heroes, although I don't like to be put in a box. It is sweet to have kids put you up on the wall.

Living it up at the Melbourne Cup.

One night I was watching a documentary on tellie and they cut to a girl in her bedroom and there was me in the background. It was so weird to watch a show on a topic of skincare and... I pop up. It's hard to contemplate just how many people watch you each night, I sort of sit back and have a little laugh. The queen could be having a chuckle on her throne at me for all I know!

One time it struck me how much I can mean to a fan when I was at a drama class just after I left *Neighbours*. A young guy came up to me and said how honoured he was to see me there as he enjoyed my work and didn't expect me to turn up at a class after I'd been on *Neighbours*. I was just keeping up my skills. Most people just think that you do *Neighbours* and keep on doing job after job, but it's not that easy, you have to work at it.

Then there's the public who despise you. One day I wrote how my car had been siphoned and my tyres were let down. Well, I guess you get back what you give! My teachers had that sometimes, and they expected it from their students, but I was not expecting to come out one morning to find mine in the same shape. Someone had obviously followed me home and decided to take a crack at my prize possession. That's cool though, I'd fixed it and it was up and running in no time. Another time I was driving to work and suddenly my car started wobbling, somebody had undone my wheel nuts. It's just part of the fame game, there's the fans that like you and there are the people who don't.

16th – 22nd November

What a week that was. Shooting scenes, hockey training and cramming all night to pass my exams at school. Talk about a hell week! But it finished on a high – with Terence, Marnie, Natalie and I making an appearance at the Beach Boys concert on Sunday.

The Beach Boys were one of the first bands I fell for as a little kid, they were wild. Some of the *Neighbours* kids were asked to appear there by Network Channel 10 so we all went on stage one by one.

At one point, Natalie Umbroglia and I had to cross the stage from one side to the other. But we couldn't go right in front of the band, so we thought we'd tiptoe behind them really slowly. They were playing along, one of their numbers (they're about fifty years old now but still cool dudes) not noticing

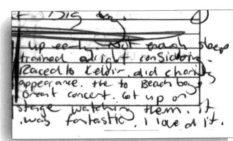

we were there, then suddenly the crowd just uproars, cheering away, but not at the Beach Boys, at Natalie and me! As soon as we peeked out on stage, about to walk across we were in full view, the crowd just went berserk. I looked over at the guys, and here they were thinking it was for them, then they slowly look behind and there's Nat and me. We got these glares from them going 'Who the hell are these kids getting the big wrap?' I was thinking 'I am soooo sorry man! This is your gig.' I was about to get down on my knees like in *Wayne's World*, 'We're not worthy, we're not worthy!' But even that wouldn't have earned our forgiveness! Nat was a big favourite with the girls as well, so between us both, we just sat there feeling really bad! We'd taken the limelight off these heroes of mine.

There was a downside though to that event. At the beginning I went up on stage about third in order of all of us. The majority of the audience were girls. There was such a huge reception so it was like 'Oh cool man. G'day girls, how you doing? Lovely to meet you all'. Then Marnie came up, who played my girlfriend on the show, and she got booed off stage. The girls were jealous of her playing my girlfriend and she came off stage very upset, carrying on about how she shouldn't have been allowed on after me. She was upset for a genuine reason. She's an actress and a damn good one too, and a nice girl, but we went up on stage in an order for marketing reasons, which were unfortunately tough on her. It was embarrassing for me and for her. I couldn't do a thing about it. Fans don't tend to like your girlfriends, on or off screen.

23-29th November

An early rise and flew up to Sydney. The afternoon was spent at the sick kids benefit (great to lift their spirits) and then had a swim at the hotel before I was off to the People's Choice Awards. They brought out a huge cake right there in front of everybody at the after party for my birthday. Wow!

HOMEWORK/ASSIGNMENTS SET	
MONDAY	Early up to Sydney. Dropped bags off at Hotel. Went to Hospital for the sick kids benefit. Picked up Tux in Grace Brothes. Had swim with Tozza, Troy, lunch etc. Cocktails before with everybody from Ten. Most Embarrassing moment of my life. They brought out a cake and all sang me happy birthday. The accords were great. After party was Brilliant.
TUESDAY	Returned back at hotel at 4.30 am woke up at 6.30am. off to Airport. Flew home with cake in under seat. Did scenes out of work Her off home half asleep. Got flowers from channel ten over then went to Grans half a sleep. Watched Neighbours had dinner then I had to sleep.
WEDNESDAY	Happy 18th Boy. Rehearsals on and that was pretty much all. Kept getting Happy Birthdays and tried to sleep while I continue with work and stuff. Finished off all my phone calls that I missed out on and that was cool.

That must have been the most embarrassing birthday ever. It was midnight by then, so yes, I was officially eighteen. Eighteenth's are meant to be memorable and mine certainly was. We partied till 4.30am.

Thursday 26th November

That night the cast met the real Ramsay Street (Pine Oak Court) residents. It went down well. The real residents are actually just your everyday next-door neighbours too. They're mainly professionals like accountants and business people. They are very tolerant of the screen neighbours making themselves at home, and I think feel a bit honoured that their houses are famous!

HOMEWORK/ASSIGNMENTS SET

MONDAY

On yeah Monday. Few scores to Release, not much though. Got home and had a hit of hockey with Tom up turf. felt great. Did lines. Spoke to Semo + Deano. Trying to organise Queensland trip.

TUESDAY

Few scores out at Factory, back home had 1 hour driving lesson. clutch seems fine. Back out to do another scene at Nunnawading. the rehearsals with Sally-Anne for Dance Doctor Zoom tomorrow. Went all right but bit nervous I guess.

WEDNESDAY

Oh here we go. The extras were really cool and got into it aswell. The Dance seem to go quiet well but I was caught up with Scott for the first time in ages. off home and had a great training up the turf in the steamy weather.

THURSDAY

end of year getaway trip with my mates in the Combi van

Friday 27th November

Hockey game was cancelled. When am I going to fit my training in? Flew up to Coolangatta, Queensland with Natalie for the Gold Coast Music Awards being telecast on Channel 10. The publicists knew I am a real animal lover, so they did a photo shoot at Seaworld of me in the pool with the dolphins. Bonus! Back in the water, my second home. The dolphins befriended me, I held on to their fins and they took me for a ride. Dolphins are amazing.

Wednesday 2nd December

That particular scene with the school dance (Dance Doctor Zoom) required a lot of extras, but they are also required in the coffee shop, on location, as mailmen, anywhere, they are an integral part of a scene. They're also required to perform in a professional manner, preferably not looking at the camera! You do get some nightmares, so it's nice to come across some who take their job seriously, makes everyone's job easier.

Friday 4th December

Woke up at 4.30am, taxi to airport off to Sydney. Did promos... Delayed at airport... had to be at work in twenty mins. Impossible you think – ah ha...

It was the last day of filming for the year, in my first year on the show. 1992. I'd been flown to Sydney to record some promos, that is previews, to be screened over the summer break on Australian TV Network Channel 10. I was filmed sliding into a pool, generally looking like I'm having a good time.

Cool. No problem. Pity about the weather though. Sometimes, you have to do things like when it's completely freezing and pretend you're having a great time. It wasn't that bad this time, but unlucky for us Sydney was raining, there were floods everywhere. And on this particular day I had to get back to Melbourne to do some scenes, the final

FRIDAY

Woke up at 4:30am taxi to Airport off to Sydney. Did Promos sliding down a slide And other publicity stuff. Delayed at Airport due to rain with Adam Digby. Finally got to Melbourne. Had to be at work in 20 mins. Impossible you think. Ah Ah. There was a helicopter

COMMENTS (Parent/Teacher): waiting for us yeah, yeah yeah. It was great Good view. Got to work on time. Went home, went to Ben Geuro's farewell and Hockey fun raiser. Dragged Scott, Felice, Julie,

PARENT'S SIGNATURE: ok, left about 1:30.

scenes for the year! After today there would be no more crew working and it's a tight schedule, costing thousands of dollars an hour for production, so I just had to get back. But, big problem, there was no way of getting there. The planes were all delayed. There were just no planes flying at all. I was running really late and my bosses were getting anxious.

So here I was waiting for a miracle with, funnily enough, the weatherman from the Melbourne news, trying to get back to present the forecast, with now under half an hour to get to work. The Premier of Victoria was walking around the airport too, looking very worried, must have been missing a party somewhere, anyway, then after about three hours, already two hours late, I got on a plane, thinking 'Great, I'll be there soon'. We got half way to Melbourne and had to turn around and fly back to Sydney because the plane had mechanical difficulties. Just wasn't my day! So back to the airport I go, mobile phone in hand ringing hot with *Neighbours* 'Where are you?' I was like, 'Oh no, it's all my fault, the whole set are relying on me to get back.

I eventually got to Tullamarine Airport in Melbourne. I had twenty minutes to be at work, but it would take too long by car to make it to the set, so I got a call telling me I would be picked up by a helicopter. I thought cool. Haven't done that before. Here's my chance! It landed right on the tarmac of the airport where everyone could see so there were all these people watching the red carpet treatment. The weather man got a ride too – to experience the weather up there first hand!

We took ten minutes to fly to the studio. It landed right outside the set. Everyone was sitting there waiting, they all knew I was coming on a helicopter. It was like 'Out the way, I'm coming through'. I ran to wardrobe, changed in five minutes and was on set doing a scene within fifteen minutes of landing. Before long it was finished. A wrap for the year. The full treatment was quite a nice experience. Thanks Reg (Grundy).

At seventeen years old it was pretty exciting! That was the biggest thrill I can remember while working on *Neighbours*.

"A" GRADE MOTOR SCHOOL

NORTH 435 1202
EAST 890 7447
WEST 435 1899

MANUALS & AUTOMATICS

MANUAL & AUTO CARS, TRUCKS & BUS, HEAVY & ENDORSEMENTS

I originally taught myself how to drive in the family's little mini

8:50am Driving lesson.
remind Linda. Good luck
Dan ☺

Monday 7th December

I got my license today. I was pretty nervous but the instructor was cool. Overall it went well. Phew! Had a few goes with reverse parking and couldn't quite make it, but didn't go through any red lights! The instructor was shaking like mad, I figured he had a nervous disorder – well, he did after today anyway.

There was no more needing a driving supervisor. It reminded me of the time when Rick put a dummie in the car to look like a driving supervisor. It was so funny. I wanted to borrow the dummie myself and give it a go!

Like Rick, I can't say I have a clean driving record I'm afraid. When my mate Deano bought a new sports car I wanted to give it a test drive. It was my first time in a sports car and I'm afraid, I lost it. I was herbing down a hill in the Melbourne suburbs and was caught out in a big way. I am a bit of a lead-foot. That's why I've especially had four-wheel drives, those cars tend to slow me down.

Strangely enough this all happened at the same time as Rick was charged with 'reckless driving' and lost his licence.

Rick ignored Lou's safe car special and opted for his dream car – a hotted-up Escort. Then he decided to race Lenny and Briggs, which ended in Briggs smashing into a telegraph pole and dying. Cody tried to slow Rick down but he wouldn't listen.

It was not often that the show allowed you to really work with some meaty storylines. That's why it is my favourite scene. There was drink driving, speeding and not wearing seat belts all involved. It was showing how you can get pushed into these things with a bit of peer group pressure. There was a lot of crying on the day. They were very intense scenes so by the end of the day, after six hours' work, Peta and I just had a mad headache.

I can't say I've ever madly raced another driver like that car crash you'll be glad to know, oh, except with Peta, who played Cody! Peta was the coolest girl, a very talented musician and a very sweet and sensitive person to have around. I miss our scenes together.

A long day and a heavy headache.

That was the only one time Lou warned Rick against risky business. In real life, Tom and I are great mates. He is a lovely man. You can always have a laugh with him and he's very down to earth. He's actually a greenie like myself. He's involved in protesting against nuclear testing as he once lived on Christmas Island, which was a nuclear testing base.

Every night after we'd finish shooting we used to race each other on the freeway all the way home, we lived about five minutes from each other. It took about half an hour's drive from from work to get home so he was great company. I always used to win, it was like who could beat all the traffic first. He loves to drive. The drive home got really boring after he left.

Isn't she lovely!

The rest of the week was just another day at the office and visiting my first home, Mount Martha with my best mate Deano.

Friday 11th December

The shifty we pulled, getting into a club for free, was, I'm afraid, becoming quite a routine of ours. The summer holiday in a few weeks was about to be scamming at its best.

1993

After my first year on *Neighbours* where I'd tackled Year 12 and state-level hockey as well, I desperately needed to get away with my mates on a holiday, and where better than sunny Surfers Paradise in Queensland? On that holiday I met someone who changed my life.

The day after Christmas my mates and I flew up to the Gold Coast. We began at Lennox Head.

My mates could tell you a story or two about their memories of the holiday.

THE INSIDE STORY
MY MATE STUART CAMPBELL

We spent a week in a hotel at Surfers Paradise and it was only then that I realised how people treat celebs. It's unbelievable. It was a whole new world. We'd get off the airplane and people would say, 'there's Rick Alessi,' and come up for autographs. We'd want to go out for the night so we'd ring up a club and pretend we were someone from *Neighbours* publicity, 'We've got one of the guys in town, we were wondering whether you'd look after him for the night, him and three of his mates.' 'Yeah for sure.' We'd get free drinks all night, and the managers would always suck up to him. It was hilarious, and all the girls would come up to him. We didn't have to do one thing in our hotel room. We had a constant stream of girls coming up and they'd do the dishes, make our bed, tidy up and we'd be sitting back having a beer and laughing, saying 'This is unbelievable Dan!' Then we'd walk out on our balcony on the eleventh floor and there were people with binoculars and cameras waiting for him to walk out on the balcony. That was really weird. All the girls were coming up to our room from nowhere, all the fourteen-year olds knocking on the door and running off, hiding around the corner with a camera to see who came out. We used to think up stories, like 'I'm coming on the show as Dan's brother next month, you haven't seen it yet'. It used to work a treat.

Another day on the road

Today I was almost killed. The four of us were riding around Surfers on the skateboards, trailing behind the bikes as normal, when a motor bike pulled up. Mmm, looked tempting. The guy didn't seem to know who I was. He said to me 'hold on to the back of the bike' so I held on and went flying off. He went slowly and then got quicker and quicker. It was the long straight road heading towards Seaworld *and he kept going faster. I started to get speed wobbles, and then I lost it and came off. As I did, an armoured truck passed. I rolled away from the* truck, giving my mates a view that looked like I'd been wiped out. Ouch. Bloody hurt. Squinting, I looked up and saw the expression on the guys' faces. They thought I was run over, dead. Nope, six lives to go. Scabs all over me. They'll kill me when I get back to* Neighbours, *with my face looking like this. How are they going to cover them up? They've managed to cover my black eyes before, but this time, I've stuffed up. Well, at least the guys haven't shaved my eyebrows off while I'm asleep like they keep threatening to!*

THE INSIDE STORY
TOM

Dan surfs with a lot of energy, like everything he does, but he's not the greatest surfer, he always ends in a stack. We usually just sit out on our boards and swim with the dolphins.

Revenge of the flushed frog!

My mates would tell you how our gang have always loved chatting to a lot of girls. But that was all about to change for me, when I found *my* girl.

Dan was always the smooth talker. A lot of the girls just fell head over heels for him because he was so good-looking. I'd never go for the good-looking one because I knew he was going to get her anyway, so I'd go for her best friend.

Dan does hold the world record for the most kisses on New Year's Eve. We were about fifteen when we went to Torque. We were on the beach for the night and he was going around kissing as many girls as he could and counting. He stopped and said 'I'm stopping now because I've found a number that I like – 69.'

The troublemakers!

Fighting

My mates always know they'll be in for a rough night when we go out because I usually attract a few fights. I'm usually alright when they talk about me, but I hate hearing them bad mouth my friends. Tom and I quite often end up in brawls. One time a fight got so out of hand I ended up being hit from behind and found myself down on the revolving dance floor, spinning around with lights flashing, people staring down at me and my shirt torn off. We just mind our own business, but that's just the pub scene. Tom, Troy and myself tore into them that night. You certainly learn to look

A smile on both cheeks!

Dan doesn't get upset, no matter what they say, but he doesn't like blokes physically pushing him around. He can be fiery, Dan's the sort of person who'll take so much and then he'll snap. There's only so much fighting you can take. There's been times when pretty much a whole pub has been on to us. One time I said, 'OK, last beers fellas', just about to go and I turn around and there's Dan standing up to this big bloke going 'what's your problem?' Another guy came from the side and all I saw was this hand from above go bang, and bop him one. The bouncers actually stuck up for the blokes saying it was their pub and not to come back.

after yourself. The one thing I never wanted to give up by being on the show was going wherever I liked. I like bands in pubs and so I put up with the attention because that's where I want to be. I have no intentions of changing.

Here we are chair-surfing. Don't try this at home!

Donna

A few days into the holiday, on the 29th December to be exact, it happened. I Met Donna.

We were in a bar and I noticed a very pretty girl. We just started talking simultaneously and hit it off within minutes. I thought she had such an energy about her.

From that day on she joined our gang and we holidayed together. I recorded everything.

Around the 5th January we headed up to Byron Bay, a beautiful coastal town north of Sydney, it's almost like an alternative, hippyish area which is a popular tourist attraction because of its stunning beaches and coastline. A bit like *Home and Away*.

3 January

7.30 Last day in Surfers'
8.00 Paradise and still to
8.30 date we've got away
9.00 with having 5 people
9.30 sleeping the night instead
10.00 of paying for just 2.
10.30 Just did the usual.
11.00 Surfed mucked around
11.30 with the boys and more
12.00 surfing. Went to Cocktails
12.30 and Dreams. Showed I.D
1.00 four times in as many
1.30 minutes. All to get into
2.00 the V.I.P. room. Great! Aftet
2.30 Had some free drinks then
3.00 moved onto Echo Beach
3.30 with Everyone. Stu tried to
4.00 pick the English chick again.
     again. I went home early

8 January

7.30 Last day before Donna
8.00 comes down from
8.30 Surfers. Went down
9.00 to Kings beach once
9.30 again more surfers
10.00 this time. Oh well
10.30 still pretty cool
11.00 surf. Got home and
11.30 just ~~fucked~~ around
12.00 for a while. During
12.30 the night I just
1.00 drank with boys on
1.30 the beach. A cute
2.00 breeze was blowing
2.30 now I had to put
3.00 on extra warm
3.30 clothing. Couldn't stop
4.00 thinking about
4.30 Donna. Thank god
5.00 she's turning up
5.30 tomorrow. Can not wait

1 January

8.00 Today's the day
8.30 I have been hanging
9.00 for. Not another girl
9.30 has crossed my mind
10.00 since I've met Don. But
10.30 knowing what people seem
11.00 to think about people like
11.30 me' they won't believe me.
12.00 But today diary I can
tell you it's true, and
a great feeling. Donna

2 January

12.30 a bloody tastic night
1.00 with Donna. We didn't
1.30 get much sleep, but thats
2.00 nothing strange. Today
2.30 We headed off the
3.00 Kings Beach to show off
3.30 'our beach' to the girls.
4.00 They loved it like everyone
4.30 else. Played some beach
5.00 cricket and had a ball.

10 January

3.30 captain who,
4.00 where and what I
4.30 knew about Donna to
5.00 them. I haven't known
5.30 her for a great deal of time,
6.00 but because we've spent
6.30 every second we had together
7.00 it feels that I have known
7.30 her for years. I hope
she takes her job in Melb.

13 January

12.30 lunch first, then
1.00 surfed this beach which
1.30 had a circular rip. crazy
2.00 stuff. Had to save some
2.30 chick out in the water
3.00 yelled help'. I thought
3.30 here we go. Chucked her
4.00 on the board infront of
4.30 me and and tried to surf
5.00 in. Almost got her to shore
5.30 then handed off to the
6.00 surf lifesavers. Huge waves
though. Went home and

15 January

8.00 It's our last day
8.30 in the house. A big night
9.00 planned with the boys
9.30 and girls. But the day
10.00 was still to come. The
10.30 girls decided they wanted
11.00 to suntan so, the fellas
11.30 sorry the legends and me
12.00 got into the car, did some
12.30 4-wheel driving to get to
1.00 this secluded beach and
1.30 stopped there. Walking on
2.00 the beach the sun got to us
2.30 Jack and I though our toes
3.00 on the beach and jumped
3.30 in starkers. The others
4.00 soon followed. We had
4.30 the best time just surfen
5.00 the waves. Got home told
5.30 the rest of the crew what we
6.00 did and they thought we were
6.30 off our tree. All the kids from
7.00 Lennox were around including Marks
7.30 three girlfriends. I had a few beers.
but Donna and I just wanted
to go to bed to be alone. Great stay

18 January

7.30 First day at work
8.00 and who's up first. Good
8.30 ol Dan. Great to
9.00 see everyone again.
9.30 Had Rehearsal scenes
10.00 involving Rick Auntie
10.30 margaret and he
11.00 scams his way out
11.30 having her here to baby-
12.00 sit him. I finished
12.30 work in the arvo and
1.00 went home for a
1.30 run. Must get fit for
championships. Soon

9 February

2.00 to the movies. We
2.30 saw A few
3.00 good men' after miss-
3.30 ing out on tickets
4.00 for another film. Donna
4.30 for some reason looked
5.00 and was absolutely
5.30 sensational. The
6.00 feelings I had for her
6.30 were, like, wow. Unfortunately
7.00 afterwords we sort of went
7.30 cold but it was soon
resolved. Thank god.

25 February

7.30 Went to school in
8.00 the morning. Trying
8.30 to cook and still what
9.00 the hell was going
9.30 on. I do feel I don't
10.00 belong. I'm not sure
10.30 if people are staring
11.00 because of who I
11.30 am or because what
12.00 the hell am I doing
12.30 here. I really don't
1.00 know. Went to earth
1.30 afterwards and
2.00 scenes went well.
2.30 Went to Miss Glings
3.00 and afterwords the

23 January

7.30 Well now that Donna's
8.00 finally in Melbourne and
8.30 I'm in bloody Canberra
9.00 I guess I better get
9.30 this job over with.
10.00 came back from S-1
10.30 down to draw with
11.00 A.C.T. close match but
11.30 it was our first for

14 February

Valentines Day
8.00 And well I finally have
8.30 someone to celebrate it
9.00 with. As Donna gave
9.30 me a pair of silk
10.00 boxer shorts and cool
10.30 teddy. Dean was
11.00 bringing me back her
11.30 present. I had no idea
12.00 what he was going
12.30 to get. It ended up
1.00 being a teddy in a
1.30 plastic box. We left
2.00 back for the city
2.30 around 2' pm. Dean
3.00 and I said our
3.30 goodbyes. Damn. and
4.00 Dean dropped me off
4.30 at my place. I had
5.00 an hour to pack and
5.30 then mr / misses Stretton
6.00 picked me up to go to the
6.30 airport. Alright trip I guess.

24 February

saw he
while. Anyway
I'm still going round
like a imwell deed fly
telling everyone how
great Donna is.
Went to Rehsals
after that and

70

8 March

We flew to Sydney to shoot the scene where Debbie and Rick were looking for Michael who ran away. Rick saw the effects of drugs on kids there.

I've seen the effect of drugs on kids too, especially the stars who are on a low and need a quick high in between all the excitement the business can offer.

Personally I wouldn't touch drugs. I'm a control person, but that's just me. I don't like being out of control. I go more insane being out of control than I would being on anything, so it's not worth it. I haven't tried anything and don't really want to.

Everyone has a release from pressure... I choose exercise. I guess I've always survived through fitness. It's good enough for me. It's a fitness of body and mind. It's weird for me not to exercise, I don't think about it. It's just in my head to 'Go and do it'. It's the discipline of taking control over my body and mind. I don't see how you gain control by willingly losing it. To have power over your mind and body is to work on it, to keep fit and not destroy it.

8.30 Start about 10:00
9.00 while everyone
9.30 was up and working.
10.00 Went for a run
10.30 and then for a surf
11.00 Great place Manly.
11.30 Everything seemed
12.00 fresh and amazing. I
12.30 think the sea air
1.00 inspired people to
1.30 get up and go. Surf
2.00 was fabulous but
2.30 then isn't it I had
3.00 for working. We had
3.30 a one shot under in front
4.00 of the Harbour bridge
4.30 and opera house but
5.00 it went well. Other
5.30 shots and scenes also
6.00 were good but was
6.30 having life without Dan
7.00 Did Radio interview with
7.30 2 Day FM. Went well. Great
experience.

7.30 Woke up. Dana brought
8.00 me coffee black and
8.30 boiling. We messed the
9.00 bed then we stuff up
9.30 cream and the coffee
10.00 went cold. I woke up
10.30 drinking from her lips,
11.00 her kisses soft and
11.30 tender and I gave up
12.00 the world just to see
12.30 her smile.
1.00 Went to St. Kilda
1.30 and had a look around
2.00 at some shops and
2.30 had an ice cream. Draped
3.00 into Rachel Blake
3.30 and then we headed
4.00 off to my place. But
4.30 first we went to
5.00 Royal Park and just

19th March

Tonight was the Logie Awards, where I always have a great time. It is very glamorous, everyone's dressed up to the hilt. It's the awards night and it feels great to be a part of it, I have to admit. All the celebrities are together. We have fun and muck around in the audience. What is seen on TV is everyone behaving themselves but half the time we're throwing bread at each other across the *Neighbours* table and just mucking around. We tend to meet each other individually through different appearances or celebrity charities anyway, and we know who each other are so we just become instant friends. That's the funny thing about the industry. You go through the same things together, you understand the exclusive sort of occupation, that's why we always

It was great while it lasted.

hang out. People are always saying, 'Why do you two hang out?' It's just because this is now our life and no other life compares to it unless someone else goes through it as well. It's weird. That night I mingled with mates like Dieter Brummer, (Shane, *Home and Away*). We originally met through a photo shoot for an article in a magazine. We ring each other up once in a while and say 'G'day, How

are you going?' He's a good man. He has a girlfriend, hate to tell you, but she is a very nice girl, she's a non-actress, (whatever category that makes you, hate to say 'a normal person'). He's so easy going and very much the 'boy next door', so much so he could have been a 'neighbour' too!

20-21st March

Things weren't looking good with Donna and me.

Jealousy over kissing scenes and attention from other girls was starting to cause trouble.

I was pretty 'head over heels' in love. At eighteen years old and experiencing 'first love' I couldn't help but express my feelings in my diary.

THE INSIDE STORY
DIETER BRUMMER
(SHANE, *HOME AND AWAY*)

Dan's a bit of a fast talker, he's always got some sort of scam up his sleeve. Anything where he can get something for nothing. I guess that's why Dan and I are fairly good friends because we're both very similar in that respect. I'm always looking out for the 'Scam of the year'.

We met at the TV Hits photo shoot that I went down to Melbourne for, and we became friends. It's always funny to hear 'Dan against Dieter', you just laugh at it and think 'Oh yeah, one of those bloody competitions', it's ridiculous. I never take notice of any of that sort of stuff. There's never any rivalry of any sort, we're not in it to try and beat someone else, we're just there to do a job.

I think Rick is a much nicer guy than Dan. Dan is a lout, a real sweetheart.

He always has a gag up his sleeve. A lot of people take themselves too seriously in the industry and that's why I like Dan, he just has a bit of fun.

He needs to grow a couple of feet, I'm 5'10", he's a little bit shorter than the rest of us. I call him 'half pint'.

7.30 I was standing
8.00 with Deano and Bell came
8.30 over and Danced I think
9.00 Donna came over and
9.30 and, well I Don't know
... I wouldn't dream
10.30 of doing anything behind
10.30 Donas back. Anyway she
Stormed off telling me
12.00 to get out her life forever
12.30 had no idea at all.
... I was going A-wall
1.30 did nothing and Dan
was convinced I did some-
thing. After a great deal
3.00 of talking and crying

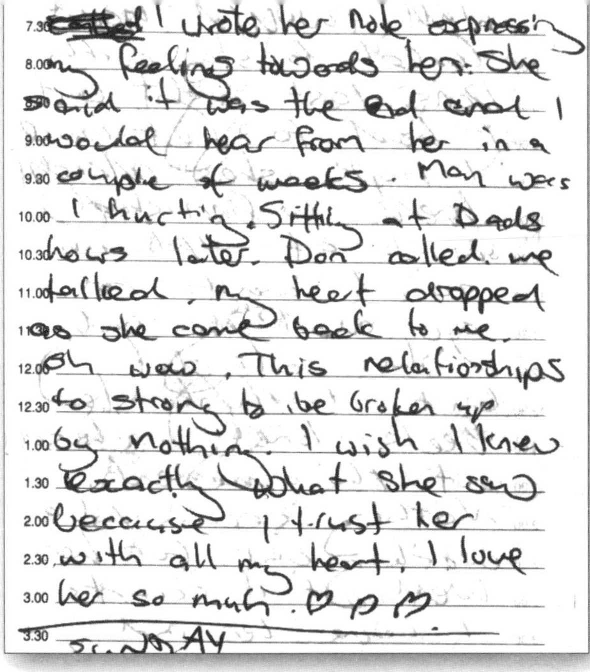

(handwritten diary, left page)

7.30 ... I wrote her note expressin'
8.00 my feeling towoods her. She
said it was the end and I
9.00 would hear from her in a
9.30 couple of weeks. Man was
10.00 I hurtin. Sittin at Dads
10.30 hours later. Don called me
11.00 talked, my heart dropped
she come back to me.
12.00 oh wow. This relationships
12.30 to strong to be broken up
1.00 by nothing. I wish I knew
1.30 exactly what she say
2.00 because I trust her
2.30 with all my heart. I love
3.00 her so much. ♡ ♡ ♡
3.30 SUNDAY

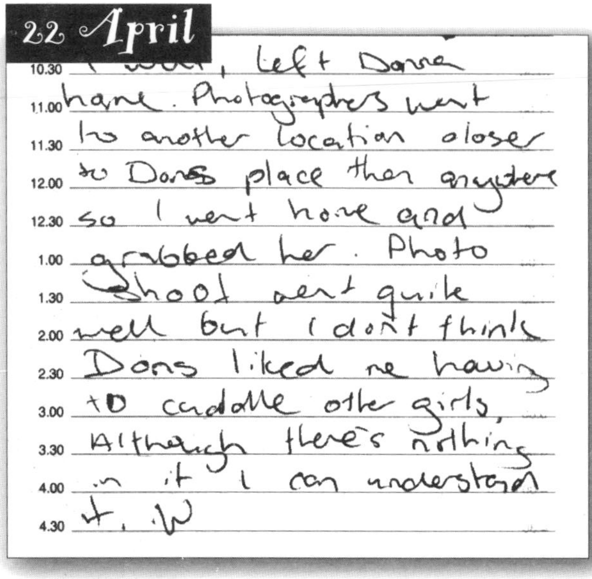

(handwritten diary, right page)

10.30 ... left Donna
11.00 home. Photographers went
11.30 to another location closer
12.00 to Dons place then anywhere
12.30 so I went home and
1.00 grabbed her. Photo
1.30 shoot went quite
2.00 well but I don't think
2.30 Dons liked me having
3.00 to cuddle other girls.
3.30 Although theres nothing
4.00 in it I can understand
4.30 t. W

22nd *April*

Unfortunately, acting kissing scenes can cause strife in personal relationships and it is difficult for many girls who aren't in the entertainment industry to turn a blind eye to it. I must admit it was easier seeing girls from the industry who totally understand the nature of acting.

I was involved with Isla, who plays Shannon in *Home and Away* and she was completely on the same wavelength. We were equals. Raelee knew we liked each other so she set us up.

Isla is a wild child. We had the most brilliant time together. She was just so full of life, it blew me away. She's just so refreshing to meet. She lives life to the fullest. She is certainly someone I greatly treasure as being a part of my life.

THE INSIDE STORY
ISLA (SHANNON, *HOME AND AWAY*)

I couldn't get over how good looking he was. We got together and found we were so similar. We're both very good salespeople, he's very astute, he could sell you anything. He is just the loveliest guy, he opens the door for you, he buys you presents. He brought me back a turquoise ring from overseas, we both have one – it's our love ring. He treats you really well, he would do anything for you. He'd ring me from the UK twice a day and we became long-distance fax friends.

And he's such a good kisser! I was definitely in love with Dan. I think we were married in a past life. I am still in love with him. But I broke it off. I broke his heart. I'd just got into *Home and Away* and I was dealing with so much and couldn't devote myself fully to the relationship. I intended the break to be just for a while and then we'd get back together, but we didn't. We're better as friends I think. Maybe we were too alike. We still go out for dinner and catch up. He's such a nice guy. The horrible guys never have a problem, but he's so nice he does.

Isla Fisher and Dieter Brummer. Now there's a stunner. The one on the left's not bad either (ha ha)!

THE INSIDE STORY
MUM

I think he's very loyal to those he loves. He really loves his family and his friends. They've only got to call and he'll come, and he would expect it in return. It's unconditional.

He is also extremely generous. There is that aspect of giving and not thinking of the returns with Dan. I think that's where I see us as being close. He's very very giving. If I need, and I have needed, I know that it's there. It doesn't matter how much it is, it's there. That's the way I've always been with them if they've needed anything it's there.

There are different levels to sex but all the hype in the media I feel, takes the real value away from it – that is, the intimacy and depth. I think it shouldn't necessarily be given away so freely because, from experience, there is more to it, so I say take your time, there's plenty of time, believe me.

So I suppose you want to know about my real life first sexual experience. My mate Deano could tell you about that.

In a word, my first sexual experience was 'humorous', and I never did get a free drink! From your first experience to when you have a serious relationship, you start realising the different emotions to it – there's more give and take in a relationship than the quick one night stand. As long as there's that honesty within sex it's great, it's fine, sex is great fun!

I think I know what love is, we all do I guess, but it still takes a long time to find it. Trust, absolute and total trust, that's all it is.

Peta Brady, who played Rick's girlfriend Cody was fun to work with. We were mates outside of work too. At one time I was visiting her place about once a week for a session of jamming on our guitars.

THE INSIDE STORY
PETA BRADY (CODY WILLIS)

There were no nightmares with kissing scenes. He'd always help me get into the moment in a scene, just by listening and being a good actor. He has a nice energy about him.

Sex

As you can imagine, sex scenes create jealousy at its worst. I'll never forget the scene with Rick and Debbie taking 'that' step. Marnie and I spoke to the producers about 'that' scene and had it changed so Rick would use protection. We understood the power of the show and that we were being role models to millions of teenagers so we didn't want to advocate unsafe sex.

It's a tough job!

THE INSIDE STORY
DEANO

We were sixteen and full of hormones back in those days. We started following some girls then asked them if they wanted to come back to a party in the local park. He found 'the one' and next thing we knew he's in the bushes. One thing led to another and... well, he came out glowing (and it wasn't the moonlight). I won't say anything more. He was a bit shy after that night. She was about a year older. I think he liked the idea her dad owned the local pub.

morning start - out of
bed at 5.50a.m. Went to
pick up Marnie on the way -
she was still in bed. Bitch!!(!!!!)
Did scenes. Paradise Beach
got the axe. Found out
about possible Perth story.
Went to school - tried to
woke up Donna (me ♥♥♥) Got
through - finally & popped her
in a taxi to my place.
       I love you darling
       Don't you forget it !!
            ever!
   Well as you know my
darling wrote the above
the rest of the day -
Most important. Donna
came over to my place.
We just worked and
played around the house.
Donna also wrote me the
most fantastic letter!
an hour hrs at given
me. I Love Her.
D. went home at 11.30pm.

5 June

This time it really looked like a break
up was 'on the cards'. But, another
false alarm.

7.30	In the morning it got
8.00	to me. I had been
8.30	hurt too many times. I
9.00	told Donna. She wasn't
9.30	fazed and didn't seem
10.00	to bother her. She said
10.30	cool, lets break up. I felt
11.00	lost and unwanted. Someone
11.30	I loved dearly and
12.00	meant everything to me
12.30	wanted out. I walked out
1.00	to catch a train. It was
1.30	freezing half way there
2.00	Donna picked me up and
2.30	fed me. We drove home together
3.00	I cried as Donna left the
3.30	street. I still think she's
4.00	the perfect girl. I went
4.30	to sleep crying. It seemed
5.00	my dreams had left me.

24th July

That day I bought my own wheels. I
was absolutely wrapped in my first
car, a white jeep. It was noisy and
rough but it was my first car so I
loved it and I still don't want to sell it.

I also have a Nissan and an old
Volkswagen as well as a Mitsubishi.
Ideally I'd like a
pale blue
Mustang.
That would
really fly!

*A couple of cars
of mine.*

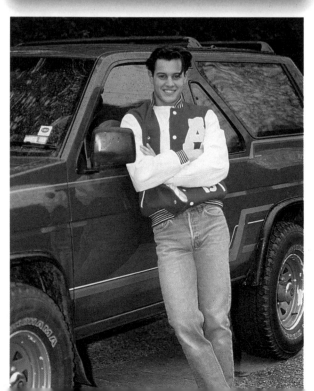

Left: *In happier times...*

Below: *Love the bow tie.*

Bye bye Diary

From the 15th October onwards I didn't keep writing in my diary. I guess I just got on with my life and kept active, so there wasn't much time to write. Yep, you guessed it, Donna and I broke up. It reached the stage where it could go no further. My decision came down to the fact there were just too many heartaches. We had some great times together but I guess you change as a person and you grow apart.

At the time I was breaking up with Donna, my life was being mirrored on *Neighbours* when Rick was breaking up with school teacher Sally. I was miserable anyway, so I didn't have a problem with putting on a sad face at work!

There are times when things might be on your mind yet you still have to go in to work and act merry. You just don't have time to ponder, you learn to think of the job at hand. I'll always remember when Kimberley's dog died. She couldn't just go home, she had to stay and do her scenes, and understandably she was a mess, anyone would be. That's why the cast gets so close half the time because you share each other's problems and heartaches. When someone has home troubles you can't help but hear about their stories in the green room.

Looking back at my first serious relationship, I thought it was love, now being some years older, I realise love can be much deeper. You fall hard with first love, especially at the age of eighteen. Although, I wasn't as bad as Rick with Sally. I just got on with my life.

1994

1994 was my first year without any other commitments on top of *Neighbours*. School had finished, I'd broken away from hockey and I was a single man again, (woohoo) but before long I was embarking on my own ventures. I became even busier once again and sorry to say, I ceased to keep a diary.

Men in suits

In April of 1994 I decided I needed a manager, not just an agent. An agent basically puts you forward for television work and fields enquiries for the next few years. After that, if you asked an agent 'What next?' they'd most probably just see what offers come in. My current Australian agent, Mark Morrisey is an exception, he faxes out updates of his clients' movements to over 300 contacts across the country.

A manager will sit down with you and help you organise how to go about your next step. That's where Stephen Harmon came in. He was booking a club for a couple of celebrities and he approached me. I was impressed with his absolute professionalism.

I visited several managers and decided on Stevo (as I call him, amongst other nicknames). He's amazing, full of enthusiasm and passion for the industry. I particularly like his aggressive approach and he always gets the best possible results for me. He's straight down the line. He'll always tell you the truth, no matter what, and he expects the same in return.

Stevo and I have become close mates

THE INSIDE STORY
MY MANAGER STEVO

I knew when I first met Dan that he was special, that this was the one I could help make it to the top. You have to not only possess the ability and talent but the right attitude and willingness to go in different directions. He's gone along with everything and is going to win at everything. There's no way he'll fail. He's pioneered the way for a lot of people.

He is not afraid to try anything, he believes he is a performer, that there's no limit for him and he is one of the few people I've ever met who understands that. There's a terrible blockage of mentality back home against diversification.

now and work together as a team. For months at a time he will sleep only every second night. He will stay up working out all the major decisions about my career. We come up against big decisions and problems every day, like which offers should we accept (if any), what do we negotiate (chicken feed), how do we proceed? Which music producer to use?

Each decision then leads to another fork in the path and a direction to choose. Every step has to be carefully

At home in the wilderness.

thought out as it affects my image and profile. People ask what's the secret to my career? Well, opportunities don't just come and I simply snap them up. Stevo would tell you 'There's just a bloody lot of hard work, gnawing away through the maze of decisions and finding the way to the top'.

Managers are there to talk about your worth as a performer. It's difficult to talk about your own value. When I do talk about myself it's usually in the third person, because I have to realise as a businessman what 'Dan' is worth in the marketplace.

It is not uncommon for soap stars to be moulded into a particular image. When I first entered the industry I let people take photos of me and use them 'willy nilly' until one day I said, 'Hang on' and decided to step in. These days I have full control over photos and my image. I feel that as it's my face up there I should be the one capitalising from it.

Along that line of thinking I came up with a similar concept to protect animal wildlife. I proposed a legislation to protect animals like koalas by

THE INSIDE STORY
MUM

Dan's amenable to things on emotional levels, for example, anything to do with the rights of animals, the planet, whatever, is a big thing. He's sees fame for what it is, a vehicle to do something else. I am happy with his development in the area he's in but I see it as a platform for other things, a way to make a contribution to the world.

gaining a percentage of money from companies who use their name and picture as a logo for marketing. It seemed logical to me. If I or any other performer were to be paid for putting our name or face to promote a product, I don't see why wildlife are any different. I feel we have to learn to start giving rather than just taking advantage. I'm still fighting for this legislation today.

I've always done what I can for the environmental movement, like helping out the Wilderness Society in Australia. I love the human race but it's just very destructive and very overwhelming and it seems to push ahead and step ahead without looking back. It seems to me that the environment is the one that suffers in the end and it's something which we can't bring back. It is our backyard and if we don't look after it now, and we're already so many years behind, it's just something that in twenty years we've got to live with that mistake. It's something I don't want to live with. It's respect for the planet, respect for the earth, respect for being on the planet. And it's one thing I learnt many years ago as far as the Aboriginal culture went, the land didn't belong to them, they belonged to the land, and that's what it is. We don't own anything and we shouldn't believe that we own anything, and we've got to pay our dues.

Please, please, please help protect and preserve the environment.

Besides my parents, my greatest role model would have to be David Suzuki. I have his books at home. He is a man with vision, who saw through the politics in the environmental movement.

It's amazing to think of the power that one program can have. *Neighbours* has a potential audience of one billion viewers worldwide. The power each individual has is most often unused. But I saw my position as a platform to affect other areas. So I offer my services to causes and charities.

Politics

There's a great deal of politics lying in me. I feel very strongly towards human rights, sexism, equality – basically that there should be happiness on our planet.

My greatest fear is the political powers losing touch with the real people, their voters.

New mates

During 1994 two actors joined the cast of *Neighbours* who became close friends of mine, Richard Grieve and red-head Raelee Hill. We'd quite often do some star-gazing of our own, in the night sky, just mellowing out on the sandy beach, just talking until four or five in the morning. We'd talk about work for a while and then the stars, then our hopes and dreams.

During the year I was offered some pantos in England but I wasn't interested. I valued my time off, I still do. I believe in working as much as you can but you've sort of got to be

happy within yourself to be able to keep going the next year. We only had four weeks off every year and I just wanted to spend that time off with family and friends. That's what is really important to me. I can keep working but you just sort of run yourself into the ground, start looking terrible and losing your friends. I just turned down the money and said 'No, I'm staying in town thanks'.

Qld Promotions trip

Richard Grieve and I decided to head up to the resort early as we had time off. We thought we'd lie by the pool taking it easy before the others arrived for the weekend, but the promotions people had other ideas – we were put to work, doing interviews and appearances.

It was Friday night, and Richard, Brett, Benji and I were beside the pool in our bathers. I was feeling a bit bored so I took my bathers off and yelled 'I'm in'. The others couldn't handle just watching me so they jumped in as well. So here we were skinny dipping in pitch dark.

Then we got into the spa and that was unreal, but the button for the spa was so far away that you had to get out and walk about six paces, so we made Brett jump out and keep pushing the button. Then, I thought the others need to be a bit more daring so I took off. I had them doing laps of this hotel stark naked then jumping back in the spa. That was too easy, softie stuff, so it was time to run where there could be people, so I leapt up and said 'Lets run into the hotel lobby.' The place was dead, so I wasn't going to ruin my mates' reputation, who could be up at this time? So we ran inside and Richard and I made it to the doors and then we stopped and hid, turned around and Benji and Brett hadn't seen that we'd stopped so they went kept running starkers in through the doors right up to this guy who was polishing the marble floors – busted! (Hee hee) They couldn't stop on the floors because they were going to bloody slip but they turned around to find Rich and I had taken off (what are friends for?). Ahh, the spa was warm. All to ourselves! We were sitting there just laughing, thinking it was hilarious. Then two security guards came walking out and we had the bubbles going in the spa, but we knew that they were just about to run out. The security guards were coming closer – they couldn't see that we were naked because of all the bubbles. So we're sitting there and they're talking to us, 'You're residents of the hotel?' and we're going 'Yeah yeah', just thinking, 'Please God let the bubbles keep going' because as soon as they'd stop we'd all be sitting there going 'Yeeks'. Then they took a look around and recognised who we were and said 'Apparently there have been some people streaking through the hotel'. We're saying, 'Really, that's no good', praying that the bubbles would keep going. Then just as they turned around and walked off, the bubbles stopped. They didn't turn around, thank God.

Farewell

I came to a point mid-way through 1994 where I decided I was ready to leave *Neighbours* and in December when I flew from the nest.

I was genuinely in tears in the farewell scene. It was not only a farewell to Rick, but a farewell to Dan. I was leaving my second family – all the *Neighbours* team. Lou and Cody waved goodbye. It was over so quickly and then we went our separate ways.

At the end of the scene it wasn't just us crying.

THE INSIDE STORY
Tom Oliver (Lou)

I miss him around the green room, that cheeky face he's got, and his sense of humour and working opposite him as a character. When Rick's mother put him in Lou's care, Lou accepted that and I think that Lou looked upon Rick as the son he didn't have. He saw in him the sort of rebelliousness and cheekiness and mischeivousness that he'd had as a younger man.

Good friends at my farewell.

Rick ventured off putting career first and leaving Cody behind. As my career progresses further, I understand how cut up he felt. I'm the one that's always leaving.

It was difficult letting go for a while, but I was looking forward to my camping trip with mates up the coast and to the next adventure ride in my career.

I learned as much as I could in that time. Three years is a long time on any job, especially one which is so intense and compact. The older actors told me 'You'll know when it's time to go' and I did. I'm a very restless person and am always seeking new challenges anyway.

I was given all sorts of weird and wonderful prezzies. Assistant director Jane Hancock gave me a garden gnome with an axe through its back. It was just the best. Jane and her husband Mark, (floor manager) knew my humour so well.

THE INSIDE STORY
Jane Hancock, Assistant Director

Nobody wanted to leave at the end of the night, it was 3am and the owners of the venue were saying 'Sorry guys you will have to leave' but everyone was standing around in tears. It was just so sad to think we wouldn't be working with him any more.

Go Wild

After my final days of work my mates and I took off for an adventure to remember. It was just the fellas. We jumped in the Combi and drove up the coast. We became quite feral, growing goaties, bathing in the ocean, sleeping on the beach. It's just so warm in Australia you can just sleep outside. It was unreal. I just let loose. I even bumped into Peta Brady in Byron Bay and we had beach parties together. We'd wake up early every day and go for a surf. Then we'd lie on the sand with our fish and chips and beers. We were beach bums. It was a laugh hanging off the back of a 'donut' dingy, you get hammered, hitting the water at 500 miles per hour, with your undies up your bum! On our way home, passing all the forests and Bob Marley blasting out, the Combi van blew up.

It was the perfect way to end the year.

1995

At the beginning of 1995 I flew from my real family nest. I packed my bags, and jumped in the four wheel drive to Sydney. I rented a small apartment overlooking the harbour. This was the first time I'd been on my own and had personal space. It was a real bachelor pad. When I didn't go out to eat I was living on baked beans and biscuits half the time.

I needed time to think and plan for my future, primarily in the UK, and put those plans into action. It was an obvious decision to move away, for my own space and to be near my agent.

I spent my whole three years on *Neighbours* going out of my way to learn as much as I could about production, seeing how things run. I was a spy. I always took notes on my findings. There is so much knowledge being thrown at you the whole time on *Neighbours*, you can choose to ignore it or absorb it and be productive. So I started thinking up production ideas.

Hang on! What's your percentage of that?

I didn't want to sit and wait for people to call me and say 'Dan, we've got a job for you', especially with only five per cent of actors in work. I wanted to be able to pick my own work – at least, I thought, have a go! My grandfather was always saying 'go and sell yourself son'. By producing my own shows I am also creating the work.

Production ideas began flowing out of my head and within about a year I had about ten proposals on the go. They vary from drama series to environmental documentaries. My brother Tom is helping to write the drama series proposal. Incoming proposals for roles gave me clues as to how a proposal should be put together. You don't necessarily need money either to start off a project, you go as far as you can with research and then the buyers decide on what is a viable proposition.

Before long, Stevo had become my business partner as well. He is very clever at the marketing side. He'll take my creations and we'll tackle the selling aspect together. There's no point in having a brilliant concept if you're not brilliant at the business side as well, that's where management comes in. The great management philosophy is that one person cannot do everything, so you need to bring the specialised experts to create a network. It all keeps us busy, especially me being the one fronting it all and sparking the ignition.

That's just the way I like to work – it fascinates me to see it all come together.

The challenge. That's the fun of it, and as soon as you start losing that, then it's all over. The big deals are like running a race and you've got to run as fast as you ever have and you get your reward at the end of the time. Money is money. I don't need much.

I wrote a proposal for my first pilot called *Hi 5* and Stevo helped to find legal protection, distributors, buyers, everything. *Hi 5* is a documentary that takes five top Australian soap stars and shows an insight into their private lives behind the public image. Kimberley and Dieter are just two mates who gave me a hand in putting it together. It was a fantastic day shooting the pilot, jet boating around Sydney Harbour and hanging out at Bondi Beach. I had produced my first creation.

Tuesday 21st March 1995

The moon is two-thirds full. The sky circles it, in all its wondrous grey and black. Every few seconds more of the moon reveals itself as cloud disperses like a child catching up to its mother.

I am now my own boss, constantly writing my proposals for shows. They seem to be going well, though only time will tell. Funny, but it's like being back at school, writing projects, giving them to Mum to check over and sending them off. Thanks to school I guess.

I flew down to Melbourne last Thursday to visit my brothers and Dad and to see Pearl Jam. They were awesome. We drank beer with the old man on the banks of the Yarra River and ventured in like followers of a religious cult.

It is now months since I have been off work (Neighbours) and it's great, no disrespect intended to the show. That time of having every ounce of energy drained from me is over.

If the moon climbs any higher it will be hidden behind my neighbour's wall any minute. It's such a beautiful sight, and the waters of Sydney Harbour are glowing from its illumination.

Funny thing happened last week. Neighbours was celebrating its tenth birthday. Well done. I received my invite in the mail and considered it for a moment. Speaking to Raelee, I discovered the crew weren't invited so I decided to give it a miss. I'm sorry, but I love the show like anyone else, but I also care for the people who are the backbone of the show. Apparently they had their own party six weeks earlier which I wasn't aware of, and they would not be attending this one. Word got out I wasn't going and before I knew it, radio stations were calling it a boycott and then the papers were hot on the trail. Why? I just figured what's the point of having a birthday cake without everyone having a piece. The crew were our base. I guess I should keep out of trouble. Everyone is important in this world, and sure the faces are the ones who sell a show but I spent half my time in the green room with the actors and half my time with the crew, they are some of my very good friends, they're all mates. Anyway, apparently everyone enjoyed themselves. I'm glad.

We all play a part

The crew work the longest hours on set of anybody. The technical people try to be on the ball at all times, which sometimes can be tiring on their part after concentrating for up to fourteen hours a day. The crew and cast work together as a team. A program like *Neighbours* could not run successfully if it wasn't a fine-tuned operation. Everyone has a specialised role from the secretary typing scripts, to the editor who finally compiles the finished product.

Because there is such pressure to churn out two and a half hours a week of TV there is not a lot of time to re-shoot, and this is why many people look down on the quality of soaps.

I found the order of scenes very interesting. When you see a coffee shop scene, all the other storylines in there for the week are filmed together. This is because its cheaper and quicker to have all the equipment, like cameras, lighting and sound in one setting than move it all off to another room. So it's all chucked in together. If that is twenty eating scenes in a row you have to do it. So we were all out of sequence all the time.

A big hug (as always) from Jossie of the Wardrobe Department

That's why there is a continuity person on set, who would tell you what had happened in the story order, as opposed to the shooting order. It's funny when a character is killed off early in the week but they've got to keep doing some more scenes at the end of the week, so they're actually dead but still filming three scenes at the end. Julie Martin and Todd Schmidt experienced that. It can make you feel really weird.

The production team is enormous, from the make-up artists, to the wardrobe department dressing you. We all need each other to put on the show.

Then there is the technical side. As an actor you need to have a basic understanding of the technical part of programme making. You need to know which camera is filming you, knowing when you're being masked (blocked) by another actor and so on. Lighting for instance, involves someone holding a shiny board next to you to reflect light, so that if you're in the shade what you're doing won't appear flat on the screen. There are floor assistants making sure the performers are in the right place at the right time, floor managers who communicate with the control room where the director sits. Also sitting there is a vision switcher controlling what is in vision. There are sound technicians who hold microphones on long poles called 'booms'. The list is endless.

Mid April

Kimbo called. We haven't spoken for a while as we're both hooning around in different states. It was great to hear from her. She's always got some problem or another to discuss, she's great. She's just so busy and in such demand these days. It's great to be here for her. She's a great girl and with her humourous way of looking at things, she'll always win.

Tomorrow I'm off again, UK here I come…

'Scragger and Muttley'.

May 1995: UK Tour

I've been on the road a few weeks now, Stevo and I sharing hotel rooms and living in each other's pockets, but there are no problems. Stevo still can't get over how I lived in bunks with my brothers till I was twenty, so sharing doesn't bother me.

Lying on the bed. Can't relax because I know I've got to pack the bloody bag up again in a minute as we'll soon be on the road . Can't wait till there's some time to chill out for at least half a day.

Probably won't make it to bed very early tonight. Last night we stayed back an extra two hours so everyone could have an autograph, and it'll probably be the same story tonight.

There's a huge boxful of teddy bears and all sorts of prezzies from fans and that's just from today! I'm wearing a black leather bracelet and a choker that were both from fans. I guess they'd be glad to know.

Last night was full on. Girls everywhere. No wonder the girls I like find my life difficult to take, being along side these beautiful women who hang around you and throw things at you on stage. It's weird, how one day you're just a normal guy, with a few girls who have a crush on you (maybe one if you're lucky) and then the next you've got thousands around you. You'd think, the opportunities are there, but the bottom line is – I'm a relationship person.

It is difficult for anyone in my position to find someone who can totally trust you.

But at the moment I'm trapped with work. It seems to conflict with my ideal situation which is being in a committed relationship. So I am a single man. That wasn't in the career brochure!

Somewhere around Valentine's Day

Attended a film launch at *Planet Hollywood*. Only for eighty exclusive guests. Walked in with cameras going berserk. On for the young and old. Didn't have a clue who the English stars were. Except East 17. Cool. They're big in Oz. Bands were dragging their minders around the party. Saw Charlie Sheen, yep, knew him. Champ. Didn't say g'day. American models everywhere. Steve and I didn't have a clue, we were the only Aussies there. It was all who you're seen with and 'ooh, what's he wearing?' Drives me bloody insane. I'm still a country boy at heart. Sometimes I feel like Paul Hogan in *Crocodile Dundee*, a down under freak in a foreign environment.

Top: *My trusty bodyguard, Jimmy Lynch, who never leaves my side.*

12th May 1995

Met up with Terence Donovan for lunch and invited him along to the *Red Nose Awards* at BBC TV where I had to present an award to Boyzone alongside Mark Owen from Take That. Stevo spoke to him as I went for food, funny guy apparently. Stevo stayed in the VIP room networking and watching the presentation on the monitor. Terence left after a while, he was bored.

I was given a scripted speech. Fun. I changed it. Naturally.

Sometimes I feel rude by not mingling, because everyone else does, but I'm the sort of person who enjoys my own company a lot these days. It really doesn't bother me, I 'll sit down and have my drink and go for a walk by myself I really enjoy that.

Played guitar in bed before counting sheep.

Where To From Here?

In 1995 I was cast in a feature film called *The Ringer*. I'm over the moon that it's a challenging and controversial main role with Alex Dimitriadis and Bill Hunter who played the dad in *Muriel's Wedding*. It's like wow, Bill Hunter is such a respected actor, and Alex and I are great mates. We were told we were the actors they wanted from the outset which was flattering. I jumped at it as it's a character who is so different from Rick, he's a street kid. Shooting is scheduled for early 1996.

1995 also marks my major recording deal with BMG records in conjunction with my band Milk. It's very exciting to be working with producers and writers on a professional scale. It was an opportunity I had always dreamed about ever since I was a child. When you finally get a chance to fulfil a dream you just go for it. It's all within the same industry, people swap from modelling to acting, from music to films, it's all integrated. It's all performing.

THE INSIDE STORY
ALEX DIMITRIADIS (HEARTBREAK HIGH)

As a mate, Dan is a witty character. He gets you in the spirit of things, there's never a down moment with Dan, unless something is really serious.

He's extremely intelligent for his age, on the ball, he knows what's going on. He's got knowledge of everything that's going on and where it's going and how to control it. He's inspired me to think you can be totally in control of your business and not let the business control you and still not drown in it.

There's a mutual respect between us, that will carry us through and give us freedom of expression. I think our relationship will affect both characterisations in *The Ringer*.

Below: *Alex and I work up a sweat.*

Opposite bottom: *My band Milk. Left to right: Andrew, Robbie, me and Sam.*

It's ironic to think I'm signing major deals in the UK and I'll ring back home to see if there are any work-related messages for me only to find McDonald's calling to check to see if I'll be back for McHappy Day. I thought, well, thanks, it's a hard choice, but I think I'll stay here for the time being, what would you do? I don't think many Australians realise how big *Neighbours* is in the UK, until they visit there themselves.

I am often asked 'who's footsteps are you going to follow now?' Nobody's – I am making my own path and moving into whichever area I feel passionate about at the time.

I actually enjoy criticism. When you think about it, knocks actually give you a push, it's like putting spit on to the fire. Criticism means you have to work at something harder, to prove them wrong. Being told 'You can't do that', makes me want to do it more. If they don't want me to do it they should say 'Go for it', and then I'd be bored!

I'm just another face really. I hope to promote and produce and be productive by bringing more shows and more educational programs to television and creating more work for the industry. Basically that's the nice thing that comes out of it, but at the same time it keeps me in work and I'm in a position of power where I can use my mind. I had an opportunity and I took it. You've got to look after yourself these days.

FAME

I was never drawn to the business for the fame. It is the sense of achieving that brings me satisfaction – to think 'Wow I can do this'. The recognition is nice, but it's only a bonus. Everyone needs a boost to say great job but what counts is how you feel about your own abilities and achievements. Fame hasn't changed my values, it's my perception of the world that has just been expanded.

Money, once again, is a bonus. I didn't grow up with a great deal of money. We never needed it to be happy. Making money is a game to me – how much you make, whether you win or lose. If you lose, you can still have a smile on your face knowing you had a go and then try something else.

The way fame is depicted in the media is all glamour with stars having such an exciting lifestyle and earning huge amounts of money. Some do earn a lot of money, but that's only for the period of time they're on the show. They're not necessarily going to have that income for the rest of their lives. At the age of sixteen and seventeen many spend it all like it's going to keep coming in. Acting roles don't last forever.

A lot of producers advise aspiring young actors that there is a lot more anguish than joy in the business. If you want it to last you have to really learn and serve your time. A three-year apprenticeship on *Neighbours* is only the beginning. Young stars who've only been in the biz for five minutes and think they know it all are just that – five-minute wonders.

Also with the fame and success comes all the attention and applause which is a great high, but you can't take it home at night with you. That's where the old saying comes from 'It's lonely at the top'. Some stars experience friends and family assuming that they've changed. That's why I value my family and friends who stick by me. They haven't changed, because Dan is still Dan. They'd never let me become big headed anyway.

Life's there to live and I never took things too seriously even on the show. It's great to have the trips and the big parties, but to be honest, I had bloody great parties with my mates! It's fantastic to just come home and party with them again. If you let work take over your life then suddenly when it goes you have nothing.

Whereever I go I'll always be a *Neighbour* and for that I'll always be proud. Just as family gives you a foundation, I was nurtured to survive in any neighbourhood.

Just thinking about the entire *Neighbours* experience makes my body feel like it's about to explode with memories. It felt like a family was leaving me, yet I was the one going. It was time. My wings were ready to fly. The nest had served its purpose and it will always be the home of discovery. It was the training ground, three years of apprenticeship. The 5.30am wakes, competing with school, the punches, the ridicule and the fame, I gladly took. The show was my second home. Not just a show to me, but my family, my friends, including the crew who most people seem to forget. A programme which everyone worked

THE INSIDE STORY
DIETER BRUMMER

I see Dan doing very well in film, he's got that look and vibe about him, you can't really explain it, it's just what I think.

THE INSIDE STORY
JAN RUSS

He's not affected. He's the same Dan as he was when he started off. He hasn't changed. To cope as a soap star and keep straight, the main thing is your upbringing and the love and support you get from your parents and family, regardless of whether they're together or separated. If you get that, anything is possible because you've got the strength and confidence in yourself. Without that, people are a bit like fish out of water, suddenly in this world of excitement and glamour, they can get really lost.

THE INSIDE STORY
DAD

I think Dan runs a competition within himself, he wants to be the best he can be, but he doesn't want to be compared at all. The only sad part is that he only touches down when he can, and then he's off again. That's just part of the industry.

THE INSIDE STORY
DEANO

Everyone that meets him can't believe that he's a normal person. He doesn't think he has to make an impression, he is just himself. He doesn't want to be looked at as to say 'Look at me, I'm number one'. He's sure of himself, but definitely not full of himself.

He does things for people because he wants to, not for what he'll get back. Like he came and met some kids belonging to a friend of mine as a favour and helped put their bunks up because they wanted to meet him. He went out of his way to do that.

THE INSIDE STORY
RICHARD GRIEVE

On Dan's last day he got up and said his philosophy 'If you love your work then you never work a day in your life'. That's so true, not that he's got an aversion to work , but if you love your work it's a pleasure. I 'll often say, 'A friend once said to me...'

incredibly hard to put on air. It served its purpose on national and international screens and I stood by it as if it were my life. Sure, it's make believe, but if society had just a fraction of its idealism, I feel the world would be a happier planet to share.

It's funny to hear critics who dissect and analyse *Neighbours* and say it doesn't truly represent Australian society. It never set out to do that. It serves a purpose in being light entertainment, audiences watch it to wind down. It's a program where you don't have to think too hard, you can enjoy the characters, who can give you a good laugh. It depicts a fictitious street where anything can

THE INSIDE STORY
MUM

I think after his apprenticeship in *Neighbours*, he's realised there's some potential for him and he's exploring it. It's not so much a grabbing, it's an exploring, and until he gets some doors shut in his face, he'll just continue. It's a positive exploration.

THE INSIDE STORY
MY BROTHER TOM

You'll find with Dan he's most happy to get away and have a surf or have a swim – that's his bottom line. He doesn't need anything huge, he's that down-to-earth in what his passions are.

He's got a basis to be happy, no matter what. He sticks to what he firmly believes in when it comes to his environment and his friends, and everything on top of that is a challenge and it's fun and you know.

If it ended tomorrow Dan would still have everything. He'd still have his family and friends, they're his main priority. He's so successful because he doesn't expect a hell of a lot, he just goes at it day by day. He's in it for the fun.

He's a smart arse that runs amok.

and will happen. I think the critics get sucked in more than the audience do half the time!

Many people walked through those doors, some lasted, some didn't. I guess I was lucky to make it through. It's one of those things, when you start a job, in the back of your scrambled mind, you constantly think of the people who didn't make it. Living up to my predecessors seemed an impossibility but, hey, I was in there.

They left the script open for Rick to return. We'll see. Who knows? I was offered great money to stay but I was never in it for the money. It was time for my next challenge.

THE INSIDE STORY
MY BROTHER BEN

I admire Dan because he has done a lot in twenty years, a lot more than some people do in a lifetime.

Mid August

Dear Diary,

Well, homeward bound once again. It was an exciting few months, touring the English countryside, meeting people and getting stuck into work. But it's time again to see my family and mates.

The air hostesses are extra-friendly. They told me I can go up the front later for a full view. Cool! I wonder what they meant?

Fell asleep at the stop-over in Bangkok. Back again, window seat. Smooth. Goodnight.

Nice sleep. Just five hours to go. Ah ha, there's light. Look, all the way down there. Wow. It seems like years since I've seen the ocean, it's a deep blue and so calm from up here. Just imagine, all the whales and dolphins. Free as I feel up here. I hope.

A sunbeam is radiating through the misty clouds. Ahh. There's the sun, golden yellow and brilliant red. It's warm rays flicker on my cheek, yes, I now feel the presence of Australia very near.

There's the coast line. Unspoiled and the home of discovery. G'day beach. Phew! I'm ready for a dip. Hello tiny island, unique, but not alone, there's another, it's a whole neighbourhood.

Touchdown! Home sweet home.

A round trip later and I still haven't sent this letter to you. Well, I could always hand deliver it next time I'm in your neighbourhood.

Anyway, that's about it for me and where I'm at now.

I haven't been on this planet for very long but if there's one bit of advice I can give I guess it's to stay positive.

It's simple I know, but at the end of the day, it really doesn't matter what you do or who you are as long as you're feeling good, that's what I call lucky. That's what I call class.

Being lucky is just keeping a smile on your face... and being good to your mum!

Keep smiling.
Lots of Love,

If you want even more up-to-date
information on Dan Falzon you
can write to his fan club at:
Dan Falzon's Fan Club
PO Box 1722
Livingston
West Lothian EH54 6XT